Contents

Introduction 3

Features 4

Unit 1: American Beginnings

Lesson 1: Early Cultures in North America 6

Content Vocabulary: artifacts, civilization, culture, domesticate, environment, migration, region, society

Academic Vocabulary: contrast, speculate

Lesson 2: Empires in the Americas................................... 14

Content Vocabulary: border, charter, convert, empire, exchange, missionary, plantation, settlement

Academic Vocabulary: confirm, objective

Lesson 3: Establishing the American Colonies 22

Content Vocabulary: colony, covenant, dissenter, indentured, pilgrim, proprietor, rebellion, sect

Academic Vocabulary: indicate, predict

Lesson 4: Economy and Trade in the Colonies................. 30

Content Vocabulary: agriculture, apprentice, duties, enterprise, export, import, mercantilism, staple

Academic Vocabulary: emphasize, expand

Unit 2: The American Revolution and the New Nation

Lesson 5: Conflict in the Colonies 38

Content Vocabulary: assembly, boycott, intolerance, militia, propaganda, repeal, sedition, tariff

Academic Vocabulary: debate, organize

Lesson 6: The American Revolution................................. 46

Content Vocabulary: congress, independence, loyalist, mercenary, patriot, petition, revolution, treaty

Academic Vocabulary: portray, propose

Lesson 7: The Constitution and the Bill of Rights............ 54

Content Vocabulary: amendment, democracy, executive, federalism, judicial, legislate, representative, republic, sovereignty

Academic Vocabulary: define, omit

Lesson 8: Growth of the New Nation............................... 62

Content Vocabulary: canal, expansion, expedition, frontier, pioneer, removal, territory

Academic Vocabulary: describe, illustrate

Contents, continued

Unit 3: Civil War and Change in the United States

Lesson 9: The Civil War and Reconstruction 70

Content Vocabulary: abolition, amnesty, compromise, confederacy, emancipation, reconstruction, secede, slavery

Academic Vocabulary: abbreviate, summarize

Lesson 10: Growth of American Industries 78

Content Vocabulary: capital, capitalism, corporation, entrepreneur, interchangeable, manufacturing, textiles, trust

Academic Vocabulary: conclude, factor

Lesson 11: Social Issues and Reform 86

Content Vocabulary: conservation, immigration, integration, nativist, progressive, segregation, socialism, suffrage

Academic Vocabulary: analyze, respond

Unit 4: The United States in the Twentieth Century

Lesson 12: World War I 94

Content Vocabulary: armistice, imperialism, isolationism, militarism, mobilize, nationalism, neutral, self-determination

Academic Vocabulary: assume, inform

Lesson 13: Between Two World Wars 102

Content Vocabulary: depression, disarmament, expatriate, prohibition, quota, relief, reparation, welfare

Academic Vocabulary: sequence, specify

Lesson 14: World War II 110

Content Vocabulary: ally, appeasement, escalation, fascism, genocide, Holocaust, internment, liberation, totalitarianism

Academic Vocabulary: highlight, survey

Lesson 15: The Cold War to the Present 118

Content Vocabulary: communism, containment, deficit, discrimination, nuclear, retaliation, sanctions, terrorism

Academic Vocabulary: relate, review

Answer Key 126

Vocabulary: American History, SV 9781419035012

Introduction

Building a strong academic and content vocabulary is the key to success in science and social studies. Current reading research indicates that vocabulary is the major factor in improving comprehension. Research also shows that students benefit from a multi-strategy approach that exposes students to vocabulary in a variety of contexts. *Vocabulary in the Content Areas* is designed to supplement basal content-area textbooks by providing theme-based vocabulary study aligned to best-selling science and social studies textbooks and standards-based assessments.

> "Students learn new words better when they encounter them often and in various contexts. The more children see, hear, and work with specific words, the better they seem to learn them."
>
> *Put Reading First* (2001)

What is *Vocabulary in the Content Areas*?
- A developmental, research-based, interactive program designed to help students build a strong vocabulary foundation in science and social studies

How does *Vocabulary in the Content Areas* build a strong vocabulary foundation?
- Through explicit instruction, practice, and application of both content-area and academic vocabulary

What are content-area vocabulary and academic vocabulary?
- Content-area vocabulary refers to the subject-specific words that students need to understand content-area concepts. Examples: *amphibian, cellular, democracy, inflation*
- Academic vocabulary refers to the words and phrases that facilitate academic discourse and that are used across several content areas. Examples: *suggest, illustrate, analyze, diagram*

What skills and strategies does *Vocabulary in the Content Areas* target to help students with their content-area coursework?
- building associations with word anchors
- using word study skills such as affixes and roots
- using parts of speech and multiple meanings
- using synonyms and antonyms and comparisons and contrasts
- using specific context clues such as in-text definitions, examples, and descriptions

In what contexts does *Vocabulary in the Content Areas* teach vocabulary?
- reading   • listening   • writing   • speaking   • test practice

In sum, *Vocabulary in the Content Areas* helps students develop a robust academic vocabulary that supports them in
- comprehension of content-area textbooks
- meaningful participation in class discussion of content-area concepts
- production of articulate content-area writing
- success on content-area, standards-based assessments

Vocabulary: American History, SV 9781419035012

Features

Vocabulary Strategy and Reading Passages

Students practice the focus strategy with two high-interest reading passages. Suggestions for note taking and marking key information in the text also help students prepare for reading passages

New American History Words and Other Useful Words

Student-friendly definitions are provided for content-area and academic vocabulary.

Word Study

Students both deepen their understanding of lesson words and increase their vocabulary acquisition through explicit instruction and practice with root words and affixes.

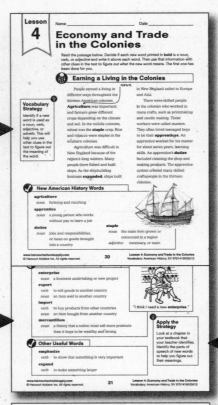

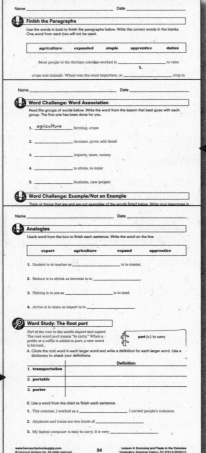

Apply the Strategy

Students practice the focus strategy with their content-area textbooks.

Vocabulary Practice

Students receive ample practice with content and vocabulary through multiple encounters with words in a variety of contexts.

Features, continued

The Language of Testing

Students build confidence and master the language of tests through test-taking tips, strategies, and practice with the types of questions they will encounter on high-stakes tests.

* Answers for multiple-choice questions in this section are included in the Answer Key for discussion purposes. It is up to teacher discretion to require students to answer the questions on their own.

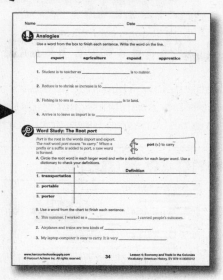

On Your Own

Students create their own understanding of content-area and academic vocabulary by answering questions that encourage thinking about the words in a variety of contexts.

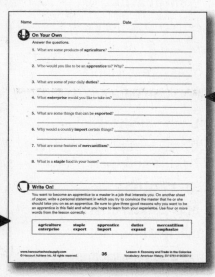

Write On!

A writing activity allows students to engage with the lesson vocabulary and concepts while also practicing key writing skills.

Assessment

Assessments for lessons provide an opportunity to monitor students' progress and give students practice answering questions in a standardized-test format.

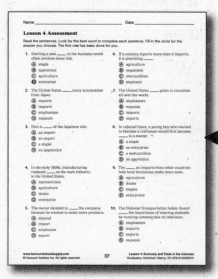

Vocabulary: American History, SV 9781419035012

Early Cultures in North America

Read the passage below. Think about the meanings of the new words printed in **bold**. Underline any definitions that might help you figure out what the new words mean. The first one has been done for you.

Moving to America

Who were the first Americans, and when did they begin living in North America? Scientists believe that thousands of years ago, there was a large **migration**, or movement, of people to America from Asia. Many scientists **speculate**, or guess, that a land bridge existed long ago between Asia and Alaska. They also believe that some people from Asia walked across the land bridge and then settled in different **regions**, or areas, of North and South America.

Scientists have learned a lot about the way the first Americans lived by studying their **artifacts**. These artifacts include tools and objects that were made by people. From these ancient artifacts, we now know that the earliest Americans built amazing **civilizations**, or developed ways of life, throughout the Americas.

✓ New American History Words

artifacts
noun tools and objects made by people

civilization
noun a group of people who share the same art, history, and laws

migration
noun movement of people or animals from one area to another

region
noun a large area of similar land

Vocabulary: American History, SV 9781419035012

Name _____ Date _____

Now read this passage and practice the vocabulary strategy again. Underline any definitions in the passage that might help you figure out what the new words in **bold** mean.

Learning to Live in North America

After crossing the land bridge, the first Americans slowly settled throughout North America. Today we call these first Americans the Native Americans. These Native Americans learned to use the **environment**, or the land, plants, and animals of where they lived, for food and shelter. Native Americans who lived in forests near the Pacific Ocean in the Northwest ate fish. They built homes from the trees in the forests. In **contrast** to Native Americans in the Northwest, Native Americans of the dry Southwest learned to farm. In other parts of North America, people learned to **domesticate**, or tame, animals to help them grow food.

As time passed, people began to live together in groups called **societies**. Each society had its own laws, leaders, and way of life. Throughout North America, Native Americans developed different **cultures**. Today, different Native American groups continue to celebrate their languages, arts, dances, and customs.

More New American History Words

culture

   noun   a body of shared traditions and beliefs

domesticate

   verb   to tame animals and grow plants for human use

environment

   noun   the land, plants, and animals in an area

society

   noun   people who live together as a group and share laws and customs

I'm just **speculating**, but I think you are in the wrong **environment**.

Fishing Poles For Rent

Other Useful Words

contrast

   noun   the differences between things

   verb   to compare the differences between things

speculate

   verb   to guess or to think about

Apply the Strategy

Look at a chapter in your textbook that your teacher identifies. Use definitions to help you figure out the meaning of any new words you find.

Name _____   Date _____

Matching

Finish the sentences in Group A with words from Group B. Write the letter of the word on the line.

Group A

1. Long ago there was a _____ of people from Asia to America.

2. Old pots, tools, and art from long ago are different types of _____.

3. A large area of similar land is called a _____.

4. The art, music, laws, and customs of _____ were developed throughout the Americas.

5. Since we did not see it happen, we can only _____ about how people migrated from Asia to North and South America.

Group B

A. civilizations

B. speculate

C. region

D. migration

E. artifacts

Group A

6. The dry Southwest had a different _____ than the rainy forests of the Northwest.

7. As people learned to farm, they _____ animals and plants for human use.

8. Native Americans formed groups, or _____, based on the culture and environment of where they lived.

9. There is a _____, or difference, between the environment and way of life of America's Northwest and Southwest.

10. Native American _____ included art, music, songs, and language.

Group B

F. societies

G. contrast

H. environment

I. culture

J. domesticated

Vocabulary: American History, SV 9781419035012

Name _____ Date _____

Word Challenge: What's Your Reason?

Read the statements below. Think of a reason for each statement and write it on the line. Write your reasons in complete sentences. The first one has been done for you.

1. A **society** could not exist where there is no food or water. _People create_ _societies, and people must have food and water._

2. Tigers and lions should not be **domesticated**. _____
   _____

3. There is a great **contrast** in the homes in a desert and the homes in a forest. _____
   _____

4. I would enjoy visiting another **culture**. _____
   _____

Word Challenge: What's Your Answer?

Read each question and write an answer on the line. Answer the questions with complete sentences. The first one has been done for you.

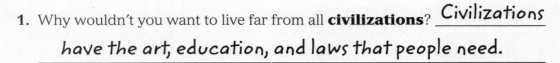

1. Why wouldn't you want to live far from all **civilizations**? _Civilizations_ _have the art, education, and laws that people need._

2. Why should you protect the **environment**? _____
   _____

3. What kind of **artifacts** show how people cooked and ate food? _____
   _____

4. What kind of **region** would you like to migrate to? _____
   _____

Name _____ Date _____

Finish the Sentence

Use a word from the box to finish each sentence. Write the correct word on the line.

migration	artifact	speculated	domesticated	region

1. Dogs were the first animals to be _____, or raised to live with people.

2. We _____ about who might have taken the bike.

3. An old comb from long ago is an _____ showing how people took care of their hair.

4. People who live in a cold, snowy _____ would want warm boots.

5. In the fall sky you can see the _____ of geese from north to south.

Word Study: The Suffix -al

The -al suffix means "relating to."

- If -al is added to a word that is a verb, the verb is changed to a noun.
- When the -al suffix is added to a noun, it changes the noun into an adjective.

arrive (v.) to reach a place
arrival (n.) the act of coming to a place
nation (n.) a group of people that have the same laws and government
national (adj.) something related to a nation

Add the -al suffix to each word. Use a dictionary to check your spelling.

	+ -al	Part of Speech
1. society		
2. environment		
3. culture		
4. region		

Name _____   Date _____

The Language of Testing

How would you answer a question like this on a test?

What factor was most important in the decision of some Indians to live near the ocean?

Ⓐ They liked the color blue.
Ⓑ They could find fish to eat.
Ⓒ They could go swimming.
Ⓓ They could bathe in the water.

Test Strategy: If the question says *what factor was most important*, ask yourself which reasons are not important. Cross off these wrong answers to help you find the correct answer. You might also rewrite the question using the word *reason* instead of factor.

1. How could you say the question above in a different way?

_____

_____

Try the strategy again by asking these questions in a different way.

2. What was the most important factor in helping Native Americans decide where to live?

Ⓐ finding dogs and cats
Ⓑ riding large horses
Ⓒ finding a safe place to build homes
Ⓓ finding bugs and frogs

3. What was the most important factor in the migration of people from Asia to the Americas?

Ⓐ the cold weather in Asia
Ⓑ the wet weather in New York
Ⓒ the land bridge that joined Asia to America
Ⓓ the wild animals in Asia

Name _____ Date _____

On Your Own

Answer the questions.

1. What can you learn from an **artifact**? _____

_____

2. What would be in your perfect **civilization**? _____

_____

3. What things do many **cultures** have in common? _____

_____

4. What animals have been **domesticated** by humans? _____

_____

5. Describe the **environment** in which you live. _____

_____

6. What makes people and animals choose **migration** over staying someplace? _____

_____

7. What **region** of the country do you live in? _____

_____

8. What are some rules you have to follow in American **society**? _____

_____

Write On!

Children digging a hole in a local park found some buried artifacts. You are an archaeologist, a scientist who studies ancient civilizations, and you are excited about this find. You want to convince the Parks Department to let you dig up the rest of the park to look for more artifacts. On another sheet of paper, write a letter describing four of the artifacts and what you have learned from them. Use four or more words from the lesson correctly.

migration	region	artifacts	civilization	environment
domesticate	society	culture	speculate	contrast

Lesson 1: Early Cultures in North America
Vocabulary: American History, SV 9781419035012

Name _____ Date _____

Lesson 1 Assessment

Read the sentences. Look for the best word to complete each sentence. Fill in the circle for the answer you choose. The first one has been done for you.

1. Our way of life, including art, laws, religion, and means of food and shelter, is a type of _____.
   A environment
   B society
   C civilization
   D region

2. Scientists _____ that people moved from Asia to America by walking over a land bridge.
   A contrast
   B speculate
   C migrate
   D civilize

3. An old pot, a rusty fork, and a ceramic bowl found buried in the ground are examples of _____.
   A artifacts
   B regions
   C contrasts
   D cultures

4. Native Americans learned to _____ animals such as horses to help them hunt for food.
   A speculate
   B domesticate
   C civilize
   D migrate

5. The land, plants, and animals that exist around you are part of the _____.
   A culture
   B civilization
   C society
   D environment

6. People who move from New York to Florida every winter are taking part in a _____.
   A society
   B migration
   C region
   D culture

7. In _____ to the booming bass and beat-box rhythms of rap, country music is more jangly and quiet.
   A migration
   B society
   C speculation
   D contrast

8. Rock music, blue jeans, and pizza are part of American _____.
   A regions
   B artifacts
   C culture
   D contrast

9. The South is one of several _____ in the United States.
   A regions
   B civilizations
   C migrations
   D artifacts

10. The other people who live in your town are part of your _____.
    A contrast
    B society
    C culture
    D migration

Lesson 1: Early Cultures in North America
Vocabulary: American History, SV 9781419035012

Name _____ Date _____

Empires in the Americas

Read the passage below. Think about the meanings of the new words printed in **bold**. Circle any familiar root words that might help you figure out what the new words mean. The first one has been done for you.

The Spanish in America

After Christopher Columbus explored America in 1492, the Spanish took over many parts of North and South America. They had two important **objectives**, or goals. Their first objective was to find gold for Spain. The second was to **convert**, or change, the religious beliefs of the Native Americans.

The Spanish explorer Francisco Pizarro defeated South America's huge Inca **empire**. An empire is a group of nations that are ruled by a more powerful country. This Native American empire included parts of the nations we now call Peru, Ecuador, and Chile. At that time, there were no real **borders**, or separation lines, between these countries. After defeating the Incas, Pizarro sent huge amounts of Inca gold to Spain.

To convert the Native Americans, the Spanish built missions in the southwestern part of the United States. The missions had forts, churches, farms, and at least one **missionary**. The missionaries taught Native Americans about the Catholic religion.

New American History Words

border

noun   an imaginary line that divides states or countries

convert

verb   to change beliefs or to change form

noun   someone who has changed his or her beliefs

empire

noun   a group of nations that are ruled by a more powerful country

missionary

noun   a religious teacher

Name _____ Date _____

Now read this passage and practice the vocabulary strategy again. Circle familiar root words that are found in larger, unfamiliar words. Write the meaning of each circled root word near it.

The First English Settlement

In 1607, three English ships landed in Virginia with a **charter** from King James of England. The charter allowed the people on the ships to start a **settlement**. Soon after landing, the men built a fort, then a church, and then houses. To honor King James, the settlement was called Jamestown.

The English settlers hoped to find gold and become rich. However, they did not find gold during their first search. Other searches **confirmed** that there was no gold in Jamestown.

Native Americans who lived nearby taught the English to grow tobacco. The settlers learned that they could sell tobacco in England and earn a lot of money. So the Jamestown settlers began growing tobacco on large farms called **plantations**.

As time passed, the English and the Native Americans **exchanged** culture and information. From the Native Americans, the English learned to grow corn, while Native Americans learned to grow onions from the English.

 More New American History Words

charter

   noun   a document that allows a business, settlement, or government to exist

exchange

   verb   to swap or to trade

   noun   a swap or trade

plantation

   noun   a very large farm where crops are grown to be sold

settlement

   noun   a community built by people just moving into an area

My **objective** is to **exchange** these leaves for gold!

Apply the Strategy

Look at a chapter in your textbook that your teacher identifies. Look for words you know in larger, unfamiliar words to help you figure out the meaning of the new words. You can keep track of these word groups in a Word Web.

 Other Useful Words

confirm

   verb   to prove or show that information is true

objective

   noun   a purpose or goal

   adjective   fair and honest

www.harcourtschoolsupply.com
15
Lesson 2: Empires in the Americas
Vocabulary: American History, SV 9781419035012

Name _____ Date _____

Finish the Sentence

Use a word from the box to finish each sentence. Write the correct word on the line.

convert	missionaries	border	empire	objectives

1. The Rio Grande forms the _____ separating the United States and Mexico.

2. Many Native Americans refused to

   _____, or change their beliefs.

3. One of Pizarro's _____ was to find gold for Spain.

4. Many mission schools were started by the

   _____.

5. The Spanish built an _____ in the Americas.

exchanged	plantations	charter	confirmed	settlement

6. The English settlers built a fort, church, and homes in a _____ they named Jamestown.

7. King James gave a group of people a _____, which gave them permission to start a settlement in North America.

8. A search of the area proved, or _____, that Native Americans had settled there first.

9. Native Americans _____, or traded, goods with the English settlers.

10. Cotton, tobacco, and sugar are grown on large farms called _____.

Name _____ Date _____

Would You Rather . . .

Read the questions below. Think of a response and write it on the line. Write your responses in complete sentences. The first one has been done for you.

1. Would you rather live in a **settlement** or on a **plantation**? _I'd rather live in a_
   settlement because I would like to live inside a fort.

2. Would you rather build an **empire** or be a **missionary**? _____
   _____

3. Would you rather **exchange** your apple for ice cream or **convert** it into applesauce?
   _____

4. Would you rather **confirm** the grade you made on your report or **speculate** about it?
   _____

Quick Pick

Read each question. Think of a response and write it on the line. Explain your answer. The first one has been done for you.

1. Which could be a **border** between two countries: a river or a mud puddle?
   A river, because it can separate two states or countries.

2. Would a **charter** give you permission to build a town or a house? _____
   _____

3. If you were a **missionary**, would you teach baseball or religion? _____
   _____

4. What do people build when they start a **settlement**: zoos or houses?
   _____

Vocabulary: American History, SV 9781419035012

Name _____ Date _____

The Right Word

Read each sentence. Look at the word or phrase that is underlined. Write a word from the box that means the same or almost the same thing as the underlined part of the sentence.

objective	border	convert	plantation	confirm

1. _____ On a <u>very large farm</u>, people grow crops that they can sell.

2. _____ The <u>goal or purpose</u> of basketball is to get the ball into the net.

3. _____ You can drive almost all day in Texas without going across the <u>line or marker between two states or countries</u> into another state.

4. _____ You should always <u>check or prove</u> that you have the right information on your ticket before getting on a plane.

5. _____ Some people choose to <u>change</u> to another religion for many different reasons.

Word Study: The Prefix *un-*

The prefix *un-* means "not." When the *un-* prefix is added to the beginning of a word, it changes the meaning of the word to the opposite of what it meant before. The word becomes its own antonym!

un + *friendly* = not friendly
un + *fair* = not fair

Complete the chart. Some of the spaces have been filled in for you. Use a dictionary to check your spellings and definitions.

	Part of Speech	+ *un-*	Definition
1. **converted**	adjective		has not changed one's beliefs
2. **confirmed**		unconfirmed	
3. **settled**	adjective		

Lesson 2: Empires in the Americas
Vocabulary: American History, SV 9781419035012

Name _____ Date _____

The Language of Testing

How would you answer a question like this on a test?

What was **the main purpose of** the Spanish missions in California?

   Ⓐ to start new farms

   Ⓑ to explore the west coast

   Ⓒ to convert the Native Americans to the Catholic religion

   Ⓓ to teach reading to the Native Americans

Tip

The word *purpose* can mean *reason* or *use*. The word *main* shows you that you need to find the most important reason or use for something.

Test Strategy: If you see a question that uses the word *purpose*, rewrite it using the words *reason* or *use*. If the word *main* is in the question, make sure you choose the most important reason or use for something.

1. How could you say the question above in a different way?

_____

_____

Try the strategy again by asking these questions in a different way.

2. What was the main purpose of the Spanish conquest of the Inca Empire?

   Ⓐ to teach the Incas to speak Spanish

   Ⓑ to capture gold for Spain

   Ⓒ to build a port on the Pacific Ocean

   Ⓓ to bring horses to South America

3. What was the main purpose of growing tobacco at Jamestown?

   Ⓐ to sell the tobacco and earn a profit

   Ⓑ to improve the soil near Jamestown

   Ⓒ to become better farmers

   Ⓓ to form friendships with Native Americans

Lesson 2: Empires in the Americas
Vocabulary: American History, SV 9781419035012

Name _____   Date _____

 On Your Own

Answer the questions.

1. What countries share **borders** with the United States? _____

_____

2. What is the purpose of a **charter**? _____

_____

3. How could you **convert** someone to be a fan of your favorite sport team? _____

_____

4. What are some **empires** you've learned about? _____

_____

5. What is something you've **exchanged** with a friend? _____

_____

6. What kind of work does a **missionary** do? _____

_____

7. What kind of work happened on a **plantation**? _____

_____

8. What would it have been like to live in an early American **settlement**? _____

_____

 Write On!

It's 1605, and you are a British explorer who wants to take a group of people over to live in America. On another sheet of paper, write a letter to King James requesting his permission. Be sure to explain your three main reasons for going to America, as well as your plans for after you arrive. Use four or more words from the lesson correctly in your letter.

convert	empire	border	missionary	charter
settlement	plantation	exchange	confirm	objective

Lesson 2: Empires in the Americas
Vocabulary: American History, SV 9781419035012

Name _____ Date _____

Lesson 2 Assessment

Read the sentences. Look for the best word to complete each sentence. Fill in the circle for the answer you choose. The first one has been done for you.

1. A person might _____ to Buddhism.
   - Ⓐ exchange
   - **Ⓑ** convert
   - Ⓒ confirm
   - Ⓓ settle

2. _____ gave the Pilgrims permission to found a colony in Massachusetts.
   - Ⓐ A missionary
   - Ⓑ A border
   - Ⓒ An objective
   - Ⓓ A charter

3. Getting straight As is an example of _____.
   - Ⓐ a charter
   - Ⓑ an objective
   - Ⓒ a border
   - Ⓓ a missionary

4. The British _____ contained India, the American colonies, and several islands in the Caribbean.
   - Ⓐ charter
   - Ⓑ settlement
   - Ⓒ empire
   - Ⓓ plantation

5. The Mississippi River forms the _____ between several states.
   - Ⓐ border
   - Ⓑ settlement
   - Ⓒ charter
   - Ⓓ objective

6. Jamestown was the name of the first English _____.
   - Ⓐ border
   - Ⓑ empire
   - Ⓒ charter
   - Ⓓ settlement

7. Mark's brother is _____ who teaches people in Africa about Christianity.
   - Ⓐ an objective
   - Ⓑ a charter
   - Ⓒ a missionary
   - Ⓓ a border

8. The two students _____ papers and corrected them.
   - Ⓐ exchanged
   - Ⓑ converted
   - Ⓒ settled
   - Ⓓ confirmed

9. I cannot _____ that the statement is true.
   - Ⓐ convert
   - Ⓑ settle
   - Ⓒ object
   - Ⓓ confirm

10. Sugarcane is grown on large _____.
    - Ⓐ settlements
    - Ⓑ borders
    - Ⓒ plantations
    - Ⓓ empires

Name _____   Date _____

Establishing the American Colonies

Read the passage below. Think about the meanings of the new words printed in **bold**. Underline any words or phrases that seem to be contrasted with the new words. Draw an arrow from each underlined word or phrase to the new word it is contrasted with. The first one has been done for you.

The Pilgrims Travel to America

Vocabulary Strategy

Use contrasts to help you understand the meanings of new words. Look for clues that point out contrasts, such as *unlike*, *instead*, or *different from*.

In the early 1600s, everyone in England was required to attend the Church of England. <u>Unlike most people who followed this rule, however</u>, religious **dissenters** refused to attend the Church of England.

One group of dissenters decided to move to America to find religious freedom. They traveled on a small ship called the *Mayflower*. The people on the *Mayflower* were called the **Pilgrims**, because they were traveling in search of religious freedom. Ten of the people on the *Mayflower* were **indentured** servants. Unlike the people who paid to travel on the *Mayflower*, these indentured servants did not pay. Instead, they would work as unpaid servants for a number of years in America.

Before leaving their ship, the Pilgrims wrote a **covenant**, or agreement, called the Mayflower Compact. This covenant said they would make laws that would be fair to all. The Pilgrims started a town called Plymouth in Massachusetts. They could not **predict** that in 1621 they would celebrate Thanksgiving with new Native American friends.

✔ New American History Words

covenant

   noun   a promise or written agreement

dissenter

   noun   a person who disagrees

indentured

   adjective   describes a person who pays off a debt working for free

pilgrim

   noun   a person who moves or travels to another place for religious reasons

Name _____ Date _____

Now read this passage and practice the vocabulary strategy again. Underline the words and phrases that use contrasts to show the meaning of **rebellion**.

More Colonies for England

In 1630, the Puritans left England for America because they wanted religious freedom. Their settlement grew into the Massachusetts **colony**, one of the thirteen English colonies.

The Puritans required everyone to pray in a Puritan church. A minister named Roger Williams believed that all people should be able to pray in their own way, however. The Puritans thought Roger Williams's ideas would not bring peace but could cause **rebellion**. They decided to send him back to England. However, Roger Williams escaped and started the colony of Providence in what is now the state of Rhode Island.

William Penn also started a colony based on religious freedom. Penn belonged to the Quakers, a religious **sect**, or group, that disagreed with the Church of England. King Charles II of England made Penn the **proprietor**, or owner, of land that is now called Pennsylvania. The acceptance of all religions in Providence and Penn's colony **indicated** their leaders' belief in religious freedom.

"Look! The **proprietor** put out a sign! Here's where we'll start our **colony**!"

More New American History Words

colony
noun   a settlement that belongs to another country

proprietor
noun   a person who owns land or a business

rebellion
noun   the act of fighting against the government or the people in charge

sect
noun   a group of people who have beliefs that are different from the main group

Other Useful Words

indicate
verb   to show some kind of fact

predict
verb   to guess what might happen

Apply the Strategy

Look at a chapter in your textbook that your teacher identifies. Use contrasting words and phrases to help you figure out the meaning of any new words you find. Keep track of these contrasts in a chart.

Name _____ Date _____

Find the Word

Write a word from the box next to each clue. Then write the word formed by the boxed letters to answer the question below.

rebellion pilgrim	indicate sect	dissenter proprietor	indentured colony	predict covenant

1. a person looking for religious freedom ☐ _ _ _ _ _ _

2. someone who disagrees _ _ _ _ _ _ _ _ _ ☐

3. a promise _ _ ☐ _ _ _ _ _

4. to make a guess about something happening ☐ _ _ _ _ _ _

5. owner of land or business _ _ ☐ _ _ _ _ _ _ _ _

6. an action against a government _ _ _ _ _ _ ☐ _ _

7. a group that has different beliefs _ _ _ ☐ _

8. to show certain facts _ _ _ _ _ _ _ ☐ _

9. a settlement ruled by another country _ _ _ ☐ _ _

10. working without pay _ _ _ _ _ _ _ _ ☐ _ _

What was William Penn called because he owned the land for the Pennsylvania colony?

A _ _ _ _ _ _ _ _ _ _ _

Name _____   Date _____

Word Challenge: Correct or Incorrect?

Write **C** if the sentence is correct, and write **I** if the sentence is incorrect. Rewrite the incorrect sentences. The first one has been done for you.

1. __C__ A **covenant** is an agreement that must be kept.

2. _____ An **indentured** worker is paid well for his or her work.

   _____

3. _____ Everyone lived peacefully during the **rebellion**.

   _____

4. _____ The **colony** in Florida was ruled by Spain.

   _____

Word Challenge: Finish the Idea

Read the incomplete sentences below. Write an ending for each. The first one has been done for you.

1. People might join a religious **sect** because _they dislike the ideas of_ _the main religion._

2. A person would be called a **pilgrim** if _____

   _____

3. A person might become a **dissenter** because _____

   _____

4. A failing grade on a math test **indicates** _____

   _____

Lesson 3: Establishing the American Colonies
Vocabulary: American History, SV 9781419035012

Name _____ Date _____

Extend the Meaning

Write the letter of the word or phrase that best completes each sentence.

1. By signing a **covenant**, you would be making a _____.
   a. promise
   b. speech
   c. painting

2. A person might become an **indentured** servant if he or she _____.
   a. enjoyed cooking for others
   b. wanted to go to college
   c. could not afford to pay for the trip to America

3. People can try to **predict** _____.
   a. the winner of an election
   b. the number of pennies in a dollar
   c. the name of their school

4. Angry people might start a **rebellion** because _____.
   a. they want to change unfair laws
   b. they have enough food for their families
   c. they respect their king

Word Study: The Suffixes *-er* and *-or*

When the *-or* or *-er* suffix is added to a verb, two things happen.

- The verb is changed to a noun.
- The verb now refers to a person or tool that can do something.

teach (v.)	teacher (n.)
help (v.)	helper (n.)
work (v.)	worker (n.)
predict (v.)	predictor (n.)

Complete the chart. Use a dictionary to check your spelling and definitions.

	+ *-er* or *-or*	New Part of Speech	Definition
1. **dissent**			
2. **indicate**			
3. **settle**			
4. **plant**			

Name _____ Date _____

The Language of Testing

How would you answer a question like this on a test?

Based on the table and your knowledge of social studies, what colony was started in 1636?

- Ⓐ Virginia
- Ⓒ Providence
- Ⓑ Massachusetts
- Ⓓ Pennsylvania

The phrase *based on the table and your knowledge of social studies* means you must read the chart and think about what you know about the topic.

The Founding of Four American Colonies

Date	Colony
1620	Pilgrims settled in Plymouth, Massachusetts
1630	Puritans started the Massachusetts Bay colony
1636	Roger Williams started the colony of Providence
1682	William Penn started the proprietary colony of Pennsylvania

Test Strategy:
- Always read the whole question and the answers first. Cross off the answers that you know are wrong. For example, there is no information in the chart about Virginia. Therefore, choice A must be wrong.
- Rewrite the question using the phrase *use the chart* instead of *based on the chart*.

Try the strategy again by asking these questions in a different way.

1. Based on the chart and your knowledge of social studies, which people were the first to settle in New England?

   - Ⓐ Pilgrims
   - Ⓒ Puritans
   - Ⓑ Dutch
   - Ⓓ Spanish

   _____
   _____
   _____
   _____
   _____
   _____

2. Based on the chart and your knowledge of social studies, which colony was started by a wealthy person?

   - Ⓐ Massachusetts
   - Ⓒ Pennsylvania
   - Ⓑ New York
   - Ⓓ Virginia

   _____
   _____
   _____
   _____
   _____
   _____

Name _____ Date _____

On Your Own

Answer the questions.

1. Name a country that built a **colony** in North America. _____
_____

2. Why might people make **covenants**? _____
_____

3. What things might a **dissenter** do? _____
_____

4. What was life like for an **indentured** servant? _____
_____

5. What might be a **pilgrim's** goals? _____
_____

6. Who is the **proprietor** of your favorite store? _____
_____

7. Why might someone start a **rebellion**? _____
_____

8. What might make people want to form a **sect**? _____
_____

Write On!

You are an indentured servant who has been living and working in America for a year. On another sheet of paper, write a letter to a family member back home describing your new home and the people you have met. Be sure to include your feelings about your life in America. Use four or more words from the lesson correctly in your letter.

dissenter	**pilgrim**	**indentured**	**covenant**	**colony**
rebellion	**sect**	**predict**	**indicate**	**proprietor**

Vocabulary: American History, SV 9781419035012

Name _____ Date _____

Lesson 3 Assessment

Read the sentences. Look for the best word to complete each sentence. Fill in the circle for the answer you choose. The first one has been done for you.

1. Peter disagrees with the members of his soccer team. He is _____.
   - Ⓐ a pilgrim
   - ⬤ a dissenter
   - Ⓒ an indentured servant
   - Ⓓ a sect

2. A group of workers don't agree with their bosses, so they quit. The workers are taking part in a _____.
   - Ⓐ colony
   - Ⓑ covenant
   - Ⓒ sect
   - Ⓓ rebellion

3. Tia and Marco wrote an agreement before they started their new business. They wrote a _____.
   - Ⓐ covenant
   - Ⓑ sect
   - Ⓒ rebellion
   - Ⓓ colony

4. Matthew agreed to work for a wealthy farmer in order to travel to America. Matthew was _____.
   - Ⓐ a dissenter
   - Ⓑ a sect
   - Ⓒ an indentured servant
   - Ⓓ a pilgrim

5. Rashid is traveling to Mecca for his religion. Rashid is _____.
   - Ⓐ a proprietor
   - Ⓑ a pilgrim
   - Ⓒ a dissenter
   - Ⓓ an indentured servant

6. Maria thinks it will rain tomorrow. She is _____ a huge thunderstorm.
   - Ⓐ indicating
   - Ⓑ dissenting
   - Ⓒ confirming
   - Ⓓ predicting

7. The citizens of Aruba have to follow the rules of the Netherlands. Aruba is a _____ of the Netherlands.
   - Ⓐ colony
   - Ⓑ sect
   - Ⓒ proprietor
   - Ⓓ covenant

8. Lisa is a member of a group that doesn't agree with all the rules of their religion. Lisa is part of a _____.
   - Ⓐ colony
   - Ⓑ covenant
   - Ⓒ sect
   - Ⓓ rebellion

9. The baby started crying until her mother gave her a bottle. The baby was _____ that she was hungry.
   - Ⓐ domesticating
   - Ⓑ speculating
   - Ⓒ predicting
   - Ⓓ indicating

10. Juanita owns a craft store. She is the _____.
    - Ⓐ dissenter
    - Ⓑ proprietor
    - Ⓒ covenant
    - Ⓓ indentured servant

Lesson 4

Economy and Trade in the Colonies

Name _____ Date _____

Read the passage below. Decide if each new word printed in **bold** is a noun, verb, or adjective and write it above each word. Then use that information with other clues in the text to figure out what the new word means. The first one has been done for you.

 ## Earning a Living in the Colonies

noun

People earned a living in different ways throughout the thirteen American colonies. **Agriculture** was important, and farmers grew different crops depending on the climate and soil. In the middle colonies, wheat was the **staple** crop. Rice and tobacco were staples in the southern colonies.

Agriculture was difficult in New England because of the region's long winters. Many people there fished and built ships. As the shipbuilding business **expanded**, ships built in New England sailed to Europe and Asia.

There were skilled people in the colonies who worked in many crafts, such as printmaking and candle making. These workers were called *masters*. They often hired teenaged boys to be their **apprentices**. An apprentice worked for his master for about seven years, learning skills. An apprentice's **duties** included cleaning the shop and making products. The apprentice system created many skilled craftspeople in the thirteen colonies.

Vocabulary Strategy

Identify if a new word is used as a noun, verb, adjective, or adverb. This will help you use other clues in the text to figure out the meaning of the word.

 ## New American History Words

agriculture

noun farming and ranching

apprentice

noun a young person who works without pay to learn a job

duties

noun jobs and responsibilities, or taxes on goods brought into a country

staple

noun the main item grown or consumed in a region

adjective necessary, or main

Name _____ Date _____

Now read the passage below and practice the vocabulary strategy again. Write *noun*, *verb*, or *adjective* above each new word.

 # Mercantilism and Trade

The English wanted their thirteen American colonies to bring wealth to their nation. English ideas about wealth came from a theory called **mercantilism**. Mercantilism **emphasized** that a nation needed large amounts of gold and silver to be wealthy. England could earn gold and silver through new **enterprises**, such as trade with other nations. So England wanted to **export**, or sell to other nations, more goods than it **imported** from other nations. According to mercantilism, a nation had a strong balance of trade when it exported more than it imported. The nation earned gold by exporting goods.

England passed laws forcing American colonists to import certain goods only from England. The colonists were not allowed to export any products that they had made, however. The colonists imported more than they exported, so they did not have a good balance of trade. As time passed, the colonists grew angry with England's unfair laws.

 ## More New American History Words

enterprise
   noun   a business undertaking or new project

export
   verb   to sell goods to another country
   noun   an item sold to another country

import
   verb   to buy products from other countries
   noun   an item bought from another country

mercantilism
   noun   a theory that a nation must sell more products than it buys to be wealthy and strong

"I think I need a new **enterprise**."

 ## Apply the Strategy

Look at a chapter in your textbook that your teacher identifies. Identify the parts of speech of new words to help you figure out their meanings.

 ## Other Useful Words

emphasize
   verb   to show that something is very important

expand
   verb   to make something larger

Name _____ Date _____

Finish the Paragraphs

Use the words in bold to finish the paragraphs below. Write the correct words in the blanks.
One word from each box will not be used.

agriculture	**expanded**	**staple**	**apprentice**	**duties**

Most people in the thirteen colonies worked in _____ to raise

1.

crops and animals. Wheat was the most important, or _____, crop in

2.

the middle colonies. Many people also worked at such jobs as printmaking or shoemaking.

A boy could learn one of these trades by becoming an _____ and

3.

working for a master craftsman for a number of years. Cleaning the shop and making new

products were some of an apprentice's _____.

4.

export	**colony**	**emphasized**	**mercantilism**	**import**

According to the ideas of _____, a nation needed to earn gold

5.

through trade with other countries. So England passed laws that _____

6.

the importance of controlling trade with the colonies. These laws required the colonies

to buy, or _____, their manufactured goods from England. The

7.

colonies were required to _____ most raw materials like wood and

8.

cotton to England.

Name _____   Date _____

Word Challenge: Word Association

Read the groups of words below. Write the word from the lesson that best goes with each group. The first one has been done for you.

1. _agriculture_ _____ farming, crops

2. _____ increase, grow, add detail

3. _____ imports, taxes, money

4. _____ to stress, to insist

5. _____ business, new project

Word Challenge: Example/Not an Example

Think of things that are and are not examples of the words listed below. Write your responses in the chart. The first one has been done for you.

	Example	Not an Example
1. apprentice	You work with a shoemaker to learn skills, but you don't get paid.	You work at a store and get paid every week.
2. mercantilism		
3. staple		
4. colony		

Name _____   Date _____

Analogies

Use a word from the box to finish each sentence. Write the word on the line.

export	agriculture	expand	apprentice

1. Student is to teacher as _____ is to master.

2. Reduce is to shrink as increase is to _____.

3. Fishing is to sea as _____ is to land.

4. Arrive is to leave as import is to _____.

Word Study: The Root *port*

Port is the root in the words *import* and *export*. The root word *port* means "to carry." When a prefix or a suffix is added to *port*, a new word is formed.

port (v.) to carry

A. Circle the root word in each larger word and write a definition for each larger word. Use a dictionary to check your definitions.

	Definition
1. transportation	
2. portable	
3. porter	

B. Use a word from the chart to finish each sentence.

1. This summer, I worked as a _____. I carried people's suitcases.

2. Airplanes and trains are two kinds of _____.

3. My laptop computer is easy to carry. It is very _____.

Name _____ Date _____

The Language of Testing

How would you answer a question like this on a test?

"An apprentice should never complain. He has a place to live, food to eat, and a master to work with."

What does this statement illustrate?

Ⓐ Every apprentice works very hard.

Ⓑ It is good to be an apprentice.

Ⓒ Craftsmen do not treat apprentices well.

Ⓓ An apprentice works too many years.

Tip

The phrase *what does this statement illustrate* means that you need to read the statement and decide what it means. Then choose the answer that is closest in meaning to the statement.

Test Strategy: If the question has the phrase *what does this statement illustrate*, restate the question to ask *what does this statement mean?* The answer you choose should be closest in meaning to the statement.

Try the strategy again with these questions. Cross out *illustrate* and write *mean*. Then cross out the answer choices that do not mean the same as the statement.

1. "It is unfair that the colonies must buy most manufactured goods from England."

   What does this statement illustrate?

   Ⓐ The colonies did not agree with the English trade laws.

   Ⓑ The colonies did not want to produce their own goods.

   Ⓒ The colonies have too much trade with each other.

   Ⓓ England does not produce enough goods for the colonies.

2. "England can become a rich nation through lots of exports and a favorable balance of trade."

   What does this statement illustrate?

   Ⓐ England imports too many products.

   Ⓑ England agrees with the mercantilism theory.

   Ⓒ England should import its manufactured goods.

   Ⓓ England is a poor nation.

Name _____ Date _____

On Your Own

Answer the questions.

1. What are some products of **agriculture**? _____

_____

2. Who would you like to be an **apprentice** to? Why? _____

_____

3. What are some of your daily **duties**? _____

_____

4. What **enterprise** would you like to take on? _____

_____

5. What are some things that can be **exported**? _____

_____

6. Why would a country **import** certain things? _____

_____

7. What are some features of **mercantilism**? _____

_____

8. What is a **staple** food in your home? _____

_____

Write On!

You want to become an apprentice to a master in a job that interests you. On another sheet of paper, write a personal statement in which you try to convince the master that he or she should take you on as an apprentice. Be sure to give three good reasons why you want to be an apprentice in this field and what you hope to learn from your experience. Use four or more words from the lesson correctly.

agriculture	staple	apprentice	duties	mercantilism
enterprise	export	import	expand	emphasize

Name _____ Date _____

Lesson 4 Assessment

Read the sentences. Look for the best word to complete each sentence. Fill in the circle for the answer you choose. The first one has been done for you.

1. Starting a new _____ in the business world often involves some risk.
   Ⓐ staple
   Ⓑ apprentice
   Ⓒ agriculture
   Ⓓ enterprise

2. The United States _____ many automobiles from Japan.
   Ⓐ exports
   Ⓑ imports
   Ⓒ emphasizes
   Ⓓ expands

3. Rice is _____ of the Japanese diet.
   Ⓐ an import
   Ⓑ an export
   Ⓒ a staple
   Ⓓ an apprentice

4. In the early 1900s, manufacturing replaced _____ as the main industry in the United States.
   Ⓐ mercantilism
   Ⓑ agriculture
   Ⓒ duties
   Ⓓ enterprise

5. The owner decided to _____ the company because he wanted to make more products.
   Ⓐ expand
   Ⓑ import
   Ⓒ emphasize
   Ⓓ export

6. If a country exports more than it imports, it is practicing _____.
   Ⓐ agriculture
   Ⓑ expansion
   Ⓒ mercantilism
   Ⓓ emphasis

7. The United States _____ grain to countries all over the world.
   Ⓐ emphasizes
   Ⓑ expands
   Ⓒ imports
   Ⓓ exports

8. In colonial times, a young boy who wanted to become a craftsman would first become _____ to a master.
   Ⓐ a staple
   Ⓑ an enterprise
   Ⓒ a mercantilism
   Ⓓ an apprentice

9. The _____ on imports from other countries help local businesses make more sales.
   Ⓐ agriculture
   Ⓑ duties
   Ⓒ staples
   Ⓓ enterprises

10. The National Transportation Safety Board _____ the importance of wearing seatbelts by running commercials on television.
    Ⓐ emphasizes
    Ⓑ imports
    Ⓒ exports
    Ⓓ expands

Conflict in the Colonies

Read the passage below. Think about the meanings of the words printed in **bold**. Create associations between words you know and the new words. These will help you remember what the new words mean. Mark these associations in the passage. The first one has been done for you.

The Colonists Against the British

Vocabulary Strategy

Create associations between things you know and the new words to "anchor" your understanding of the new words. You can complete a word anchor chart to help you create associations.

In Britain, people chose the members of Parliament. Parliament is where British laws are made. American colonists also chose people to write laws in their own **assemblies** that were somewhat like Parliament.

Parliament wrote laws that required American colonists to pay more **tariffs**. These tariffs taxed imported goods like sugar, tea, and paper. The colonists **debated** these tariffs. Some argued that the tariff laws were not fair because they had not chosen the members of Parliament. Some also began to **boycott** British goods. They stopped buying British cloth and made their own cloth instead.

Problems with Britain grew worse. On March 5, 1770, there was a fight in Boston, Massachusetts, between British soldiers and colonists. Three colonists were killed. The event became known as the Boston Massacre. It was used as **propaganda** to turn colonists against the British. It seemed to work.

New American History Words

assembly

noun   a group of individuals who are chosen by the people to make laws

boycott

verb   to refuse to buy certain goods or services

noun   the act of refusing to buy certain goods or services

propaganda

noun   ideas spread to change people's opinions about someone or something

tariff

noun   a tax on goods that are imported from another country

Name _____   Date _____

Now read this passage and practice the vocabulary strategy again. Write near the new words or mark in the text any associations that will help you "anchor" the meaning of the new words.

 ## The Colonists Prepare to Fight

After the Boston Massacre, colonists **organized** protests against the British. Citizens also formed **militias**. These citizen armies called themselves Minutemen. They needed only a minute to be ready to fight.

The British **repealed**, or ended, some laws such as the Stamp Act. But Americans still had to pay a tax on tea. **Sedition** grew stronger. Angry Americans **organized** the Boston Tea Party. On December 16, 1773, a group of colonists dressed as Native Americans. They went aboard the tea ships in Boston Harbor and dumped tea in the harbor. They dumped so much tea into the harbor that the water turned brown!

King George wrote laws to punish the colonists. His laws showed **intolerance** for their feelings. He didn't care that they wanted different laws. The colonists hated the new laws so much they called them the Intolerable Acts. Many colonists believed that they would have to fight for the freedom they wanted.

 ### More New American History Words

intolerance
noun   disrespect for others and their beliefs

militia
noun   an army made up of citizens, not soldiers

repeal
verb   to end or remove a law

sedition
noun   attempts to stir up anger against the government

"If we want this **propaganda** to work, we need to make King George more **intolerable**!"

 ### Apply the Strategy

Look at a chapter in your textbook that your teacher identifies. Use associations to help you anchor your understanding of any new words you find.

 ### Other Useful Words

debate
verb   to discuss a topic from different points of view
noun   a discussion in which people argue different points of view

organize
verb   to put into order

Name _____   Date _____

The Right Word

Read each sentence. Look at the word or phrase that is underlined. Write a word from the box that means the same or almost the same thing as the underlined part of the sentence.

debate	tariff	assembly	boycotted

1. _____ Our state has an elected <u>group of lawmakers who write new laws</u>.

2. _____ The <u>tax</u> on cars from other countries made the cars more expensive.

3. _____ We <u>refused to buy</u> that company's products because they were not safe.

4. _____ Pedro and Ali like to <u>discuss issues from different points of view</u>.

repeal	intolerance	militia	organize

5. _____ My mother said we must <u>put everything in order</u> in our rooms before we can go to the mall.

6. _____ Marie showed <u>she could not respect or accept the ideas and opinions of other people</u>.

7. _____ The Americans wanted Parliament to <u>end</u> unfair tariff laws.

8. _____ The people formed a <u>citizen army</u> to fight the British.

Vocabulary: American History, SV 9781419035012

Name _____   Date _____

Word Challenge: Finish the Idea

Read the incomplete sentences below. Write an ending for each. The first one has been done for you.

1. It is wrong to show **intolerance** to others, because _we should show respect for_ ___everyone's beliefs.___

2. I should **organize** my desk, because _____
_____

3. The candidates for president always **debate** the issues, because _____
_____

4. Harmful laws should be **repealed**, because _____
_____

Word Challenge: What's Your Answer?

Read each question and write the answer on the line. Answer the questions with complete sentences. The first one has been done for you.

1. What kind of work would be done in an **assembly**? _The people who_ ___are chosen to work there make laws.___

2. What kind of statements would show **sedition** against a government?
_____

3. What are some reasons why you might join a **boycott**? _____
_____

4. What kind of **propaganda** could be dangerous? _____
_____

Vocabulary: American History, SV 9781419035012

Name _____ Date _____

Synonyms or Antonyms

Look at each group of words below. Circle the two words in each group that are synonyms or the two words that are antonyms. Write synonyms or antonyms on the line.

1. boycott   staple

    charter   buy

_____

2. intolerance   disapproval

    debate   assembly

_____

3. tariff   tax

    organize   sedition

_____

4. assembly   lawmakers

    militia   dissenter

_____

Word Study: The Prefixes *in-* and *im-*

The prefixes *in-* and *im-* mean "not." Consequently, when you add one of them to a noun like *tolerance*, the word means the opposite of what it did before.

 **tolerance** (n.) respecting the ideas and beliefs of others
intolerance (n.) not accepting or respecting ideas that are different

A. Add *in-* or *im-* to the words below and write a definition. Use a dictionary to check your spelling and definitions.

	+ *im-* or *in-*	Definition
1. possible		
2. experienced		
3. convenient		
4. direct		

B. Replace the underlined words with a word from the chart.

1. It was <u>not possible</u> for us to finish our homework tonight. _____

2. It was <u>not easy</u> to pick up Sumaya at the airport. _____

The Language of Testing

How would you answer a question like this on a test?

All of the following are true

except

- (A) The English ruled thirteen American colonies.
- (B) Every colony had its own lawmaking group.
- (C) The colonies traded with England.
- (D) The colonists were happy to pay tariffs on tea and sugar.

Tip

The word *except* means you should look for something that is the opposite of the word or phrase before *except*. In this question you need to look for the answer that is false.

Test Strategy: If you see a question that has the word *except* in it, ask the question in a different way. Remember that you are looking for the answer that is false.

1. How could you say the question above in a different way?

_____

_____

Try the strategy again by asking these questions in a different way.

2. All of the following are true except
   - (A) Virginia's assembly was called the House of Burgesses.
   - (B) Every colony voted for lawmakers.
   - (C) Americans voted for people to represent them in Parliament.
   - (D) Parliament made English laws.

   _____

   _____

   _____

   _____

3. The colonists protested against Britain in all of the following ways except
   - (A) The colonies formed militias.
   - (B) Americans bought British goods.
   - (C) Americans started a boycott against British goods.
   - (D) During the Boston Tea Party, tea was dumped into Boston Harbor.

   _____

   _____

   _____

   _____

Lesson 5: Conflict in the Colonies
Vocabulary: American History, SV 9781419035012

Name _____ Date _____

Answer the questions.

1. Have you ever been a part of an **assembly**? Describe. _____
   _____

2. What might make you **boycott** a business? _____
   _____

3. How can you change people's **intolerance** of others? _____
   _____

4. Why might someone join a **militia**? _____
   _____

5. How might you know if something is **propaganda**? _____
   _____

6. What things might people ask leaders to **repeal**? _____
   _____

7. Why might someone commit **sedition**? _____
   _____

8. When might a **tariff** be unfair? _____
   _____

Write On!

You are an activist who is trying to get other people to join you in boycotting whale blubber.
On another sheet of paper, create a flyer to hand out to people to spread the word about the
boycott. Be sure to describe your cause and to explain why you feel the way you do about it.
Use persuasive language to convince people to join you in the boycott. Use four or more words
from the lesson correctly in your flyer.

assembly	**boycott**	**debate**	**intolerance**	**militia**
organize	**propaganda**	**repeal**	**sedition**	**tariff**

Vocabulary: American History, SV 9781419035012

Name _____ Date _____

Lesson 5 Assessment

Read the sentences. Fill in the circle of the answer that means the same thing as the underlined word. The first one has been done for you.

1. Emma decided to <u>boycott</u> a popular clothing store because all its merchandise is made in sweatshops in Central America.
   - Ⓐ guess or think about
   - Ⓑ sell goods to another country
   - Ⓒ put into order
   - Ⓓ refuse to buy goods or services

2. Convinced that the election results were not fair, Rick began to encourage <u>sedition</u> against the student council.
   - Ⓐ not accepting the beliefs of others
   - Ⓑ angry words and actions
   - Ⓒ a purpose or goal
   - Ⓓ a written agreement

3. The state <u>assembly</u> voted to raise the speed limit on freeways to 65 miles per hour.
   - Ⓐ people who share common laws
   - Ⓑ official paper from a government or ruler
   - Ⓒ group of lawmakers
   - Ⓓ citizen army

4. The members of the jury <u>debated</u> the guilt or innocence of the defendant.
   - Ⓐ discussed different views
   - Ⓑ proved the truth
   - Ⓒ showed as fact
   - Ⓓ guessed that something would happen

5. The government put a <u>tariff</u> on foreign cheese to encourage people to buy from local producers.
   - Ⓐ official paper
   - Ⓑ main food item
   - Ⓒ tax
   - Ⓓ written agreement

6. In 1919, the U.S. government passed the 18th Amendment to the Constitution but <u>repealed</u> it in 1933.
   - Ⓐ put into order
   - Ⓑ ended
   - Ⓒ proved as true
   - Ⓓ showed the importance of

7. Ron's treatment of people who don't agree with him shows his extreme <u>intolerance</u>.
   - Ⓐ difference
   - Ⓑ responsibility
   - Ⓒ purpose
   - Ⓓ disrespect for the beliefs of others

8. During World War II, the Nazi party used <u>propaganda</u> to influence the actions and beliefs of the German people.
   - Ⓐ tricky advertising
   - Ⓑ taxes
   - Ⓒ written agreements
   - Ⓓ official papers

9. In 1886, Samuel Gompers <u>organized</u> unions of skilled workers into the American Federation of Labor.
   - Ⓐ refused to buy
   - Ⓑ put in order
   - Ⓒ disrespected
   - Ⓓ fought against

10. The Army National Guard is an example of a modern-day <u>militia</u>.
   - Ⓐ group of people with different beliefs
   - Ⓑ people who spread a religion
   - Ⓒ group of lawmakers
   - Ⓓ citizen army

Name _____   Date _____

The American Revolution

Read the passage below. Underline the words in **bold** print that have more than one meaning. You may check the definitions below for help. The first one has been done for you.

The Colonists Choose War

In 1774, leaders from the colonies met at the First Continental **Congress** in Philadelphia to solve their problems with King George. The leaders wrote a **petition** in which they **proposed** that the king change unfair laws. But King George ignored the petition when he received it.

In 1775, colonial leaders met at the Second Continental Congress in Philadelphia and sent another petition to King George. But King George refused to even read their petition! So the Congress decided that the colonies should become a free and independent nation.

One of the youngest men at the Congress, Thomas Jefferson, agreed to write a document that explained why the colonists wanted **independence** from Britain. This document was called the Declaration of Independence. The Congress approved the Declaration of Independence on July 4, 1776.

The colonists fought the British army to win their independence. This war was a **revolution** because it completely changed their government. This war later came to be called the American Revolution.

Vocabulary Strategy

Identify words in the passage that have more than one, or multiple, meanings. In some cases a word can be used as different parts of speech. Understanding multiple meanings will help you create a fuller understanding of new words.

New American History Words

congress

noun   a large meeting held to make decisions about laws and government, or the lawmaking branch of the United States government

independence

noun   the state of being free from outside control

petition

noun   a written request

verb   to make a request

revolution

noun   a change in government that involves war, or a major change in the way people live

Lesson 6: The American Revolution
Vocabulary: American History, SV 9781419035012

Name _____ Date _____

Now read the passage below and practice the vocabulary strategy again. Check the definitions on this page for words with multiple meanings. Underline the words in **bold** print that have more than one meaning.

The Fight for Freedom

During the American Revolution, many people were **patriots** who loved their country and fought for independence from British control. Unlike the patriots, many people in the colonies were loyal to Britain. These people were called **Loyalists**. They helped the British during the war. Another group that fought was the **mercenary** soldiers. These were German soldiers who were paid by the British to fight the colonists.

The leader of the colonial army was General George Washington. Many paintings **portray** Washington as unsmiling and unfriendly. However, Washington cared about his soldiers. He also refused to give up, although he lost many battles.

Washington and his army defeated the powerful British army in 1781. In 1783, British leaders signed a peace **treaty** with the new nation. That new nation was called the United States of America.

 More New American History Words

loyalist

noun   a person who remains loyal to a government, or someone who was loyal to Great Britain during the American Revolution

mercenary

noun   a soldier who fights for pay

adjective   doing something just for pay or personal gain

patriot

noun   a person who loves his or her country, or an American colonist who fought for independence

treaty

noun   an agreement between two or more nations

Good job, Tom! But I **propose** that we are going to need more **patriots**!

What do you think, Ben?

 Apply the Strategy

Look at a chapter in your textbook that your teacher identifies. Find out if any of the new words you find have multiple meanings. Keep track of these multiple meanings in a chart.

 Other Useful Words

portray

verb   to show a person, thing, or event in a certain way

propose

verb   to suggest a plan

Name _____ Date _____

Matching

Finish the sentences in Group A with words from Group B. Write the letter of the word on the line.

Group A

1. Leaders of the Continental Congress suggested, or _____, that a petition be sent to King George.

2. The colonists decided they wanted to be free from British control, so they declared _____.

3. People who love and support their country are called _____.

4. Colonists who felt loyal to Britain were called _____.

Group B

A. patriots

B. proposed

C. Loyalists

D. independence

Library of Congress

Group A

5. The colonists fought a _____ to win their freedom from Britain.

6. The British paid _____ soldiers to fight against Americans.

7. Members of the Continental Congress sent a _____ to King George asking him to change the laws.

8. After Americans defeated the British, the United States and Britain agreed to peace by signing a _____.

Group B

E. mercenary

F. treaty

G. revolution

H. petition

Vocabulary: American History, SV 9781419035012

Name _____ Date _____

Word Challenge: Would You Rather . . .

Read the questions below. Think of a response and write it on the line. Write your responses in complete sentences. The first one has been done for you.

1. Would you rather have been a **mercenary** or a **patriot** in the American Revolution? ___I___ _would rather have been a patriot so that I would have believed in what I was fighting for._

2. Would you rather show your **independence** or be a **loyalist**? _____

   _____

3. Would you rather fight a **revolution** or a sign a **petition** to change a situation? _____

   _____

4. Would you rather **propose** a **treaty** with your enemies or **petition** them to change?

   _____

Word Challenge: Quick Pick

Read each question. Think of a response and write it on the line. Explain your answer. The first one has been done for you.

1. What could be planned at a **congress**: new laws or a new playground?
   Congress would plan new laws.
   _____

2. What would a **loyalist** do: support or fight against the government?

   _____

3. How would you **portray** your family to your friends: would you describe
   them or would you refuse to talk about them? _____

   _____

4. What should a teacher **propose** to a class: a new video game or a new

   project? _____

Lesson 6: The American Revolution
Vocabulary: American History, SV 9781419035012

Name _____ Date _____

Finish the Idea

Finish each idea to make a complete sentence. Write your answer on the line.

1. I would call someone a **patriot** if he or she _____

_____

2. You could call someone **mercenary** if _____

_____

3. I would call a change in society a **revolution** if _____

_____

4. If I was an artist, I would **portray** my best friend as _____

_____

Word Study: The Suffix -tion

When you add the suffix -tion to a verb such as
decorate, two things happen.
- The verb changes to a noun: decoration.
- The word now refers to an item that you
  add to something to make it more attractive.

decorate (v.) to make
something more attractive
decoration (n.) something
you add to something else to
make it more attractive

A. Add the -tion suffix to the following words and write your own definition. Use a dictionary to
check your spelling and your definitions.

	+ -tion	**Definition**
1. **locate**		
2. **propose**		
3. **revolt**		

B. Use a word from the chart with the -tion suffix to finish each sentence.

1. The beach is a good place, or _____, for a summer party.

2. The community liked Anya's suggestion, or _____, that the city build
   a new skate park.

Name _____ Date _____

The Language of Testing

How would you answer a question like this on a test?

 **What was the result of** the First
Continental Congress?

    Ⓐ The British changed all unfair laws.
    Ⓑ The colonists ended their boycott.
    Ⓒ Most Americans became Loyalists.
    Ⓓ Americans sent a petition to King George.

Tip

The phrase *what was the result of* can also mean *what happened after.*

Test Strategy: When you find a question that asks you for the result of something, you are supposed to look for a cause and effect relationship. You can rewrite the question using *what happened because of* or *what happened after* instead of *what was the result of.*

1. How could you say the question above in a different way?

_____

_____

Try the strategy again by asking these questions in a different way.

2. One result of the Boston Tea Party was

    Ⓐ the Boston Massacre.
    Ⓑ more trade between the colonies and Britain.
    Ⓒ an increase in colonists drinking tea.
    Ⓓ King George's punishment of the colonists in Boston.

3. What was one result of the American Revolution?

    Ⓐ The British sent petitions to the United States.
    Ⓑ King George became popular in the United States.
    Ⓒ The colonies became independent.
    Ⓓ Colonists began to travel to Britain.

_____   _____

_____   _____

_____   _____

_____   _____

_____   _____

Lesson 6: The American Revolution
Vocabulary: American History, SV 9781419035012

Name _____ Date _____

 On Your Own

Answer the questions.

1. What does a **congress** do? _____
_____

2. How do you show your **independence**? _____
_____

3. What are some things a **loyalist** might do? _____
_____

4. What are some differences between a **mercenary** and a regular soldier? _____
_____

5. What are some things a **patriot** might do? _____
_____

6. What might you write a **petition** for? _____
_____

7. What are some possible results of a **revolution**? _____
_____

8. What information might be in a **treaty**? _____
_____

 Write On!

You are a patriot who wants to help convince your fellow colonists to fight for independence. On another sheet of paper, write a short speech in which you talk about examples of the unfairness of British rule and the positive aspects of independence. Be sure to include your own feelings on the subject. You should also use four or more words from the lesson correctly in your speech.

| congress | petition | independence | revolution | patriot |
| loyalist | mercenary | treaty | propose | portray |

Lesson 6: The American Revolution
Vocabulary: American History, SV 9781419035012

Name _____ Date _____

Lesson 6 Assessment

Read the sentences. Look for the best word or phrase to complete each sentence. Fill in the circle for the answer you choose. The first one has been done for you.

1. The primary responsibility of Congress is to _____.
   - Ⓐ elect the president
   - Ⓑ fight enemies
   - **Ⓒ make laws**
   - Ⓓ hear court cases

2. A person might write a petition to _____.
   - Ⓐ order a meal
   - Ⓑ start a revolution
   - Ⓒ request that a law be changed
   - Ⓓ end a war

3. A country that has gained its independence _____.
   - Ⓐ must pay a fee to another country
   - Ⓑ can send representatives to the parent country's government
   - Ⓒ can make laws for another country
   - Ⓓ is free from outside control

4. People who fight a successful revolution can expect _____.
   - Ⓐ a change in their way of life
   - Ⓑ to go to jail
   - Ⓒ to be tried in court
   - Ⓓ that everything will remain the same

5. A patriot will _____.
   - Ⓐ show dislike for his or her country
   - Ⓑ support his or her country
   - Ⓒ leave his or her country
   - Ⓓ dissent against the government

6. A mercenary person will do something _____.
   - Ⓐ out of kindness
   - Ⓑ to help someone
   - Ⓒ even if it causes him or her personal harm
   - Ⓓ in order to get paid

7. Two countries would sign a treaty if they _____.
   - Ⓐ wanted to start a war
   - Ⓑ wanted to have nothing to do with each other in the future
   - Ⓒ wanted to end a war
   - Ⓓ wanted to compete in athletic events

8. A loyalist in the American colonies would _____.
   - Ⓐ join a colonial militia
   - Ⓑ support the British king
   - Ⓒ act as a spy for the colonists
   - Ⓓ join the Continental Congress

9. A person who proposes something is _____.
   - Ⓐ putting something in order
   - Ⓑ proving that something is correct
   - Ⓒ making a guess
   - Ⓓ suggesting a plan

10. A person would most likely portray his or her enemy as _____.
   - Ⓐ kind
   - Ⓑ unfriendly
   - Ⓒ honest
   - Ⓓ loyal

The Constitution and the Bill of Rights

Read the passage below. Think about the meaning of the words printed in **bold**. Circle any words that end with *-cy*, *-ic*, and *-ism*. Write what each suffix means near it in the passage. Remember that *-cy* names a type of government, *-ic* describes a connection, and *-ism* names a belief. The first one has been done for you.

Name _____ Date _____

type of government

Planning the Constitution

American leaders wanted their country to be a **democracy** in which the American people would govern themselves. In 1787, they wrote laws called the United States Constitution in order to do just that.

The Constitution has **sovereignty** over all other laws. This means the Constitution is the highest law in the nation.

One goal of the Constitution was to create a **republic**. We can **define** republic as a government without a king or queen in which citizens elect their leaders. A second goal was to create a government based on the ideas of **federalism**. Federalism is defined as a system in which powers are shared by the federal, or national, government and the state governments.

A third goal was that new laws called **amendments** could be added to the Constitution when needed. Since 1787, twenty-seven amendments have been added.

Vocabulary Strategy

Identify suffixes that can help you understand the meaning of new words.

New American History Words

amendment

noun a law that is added to the Constitution, or a change that is made to make a law or rule better

democracy

noun a system of government in which people choose their leaders and laws

federalism

noun sharing of powers between the state governments and the national government

republic

noun a country in which citizens vote for government leaders

sovereignty

noun a nation's power to control its own government

Name _____ Date _____

Now read this passage and circle any words that end with *-ive* and *-al*. Write what each suffix means near it in the passage. Remember that *-ive* describes a characteristic, and *-al* describes a connection to an idea.

The Three Branches of Government

The writers of the Constitution divided the government powers into three branches. The first branch is the legislative, or lawmaking, branch. Lawmakers work in the two houses of Congress — the Senate and the House of Representatives. Members of Congress **legislate** new laws for the nation. Americans elect **representatives** to legislate for them in Congress.

The second branch is the **executive** branch. Its job is to carry out the laws made by Congress. The President leads the executive branch.

The **judicial** branch is the third branch. The judicial branch controls the nation's court system. The United States Supreme Court is the highest court in the judicial branch.

In 1787, the writers of the Constitution had **omitted** laws to protect personal freedom. The Bill of Rights was added to the Constitution in 1791. It contains ten amendments that protect the rights of every American.

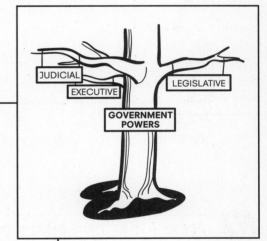

More New American History Words

executive
  adjective   having to do with putting laws into action

judicial
  adjective   having to do with the courts and judges

legislate
  verb   to make and pass laws

representative
  noun   a person who is elected to make laws in Congress, or a person who acts for other people

Other Useful Words

define
  verb   to explain what something means

omit
  verb   to leave out or not include

Apply the Strategy

Look at a chapter in your textbook that your teacher identifies. Use familiar prefixes and suffixes to help you figure out the meaning of any new words you find.

Name _____   Date _____

 Finish the Sentence

Use a word from the box to finish each sentence. Write the correct word on the line.

legislate	republic	amendment	executive	judicial

1. The _____ branch carries out the nation's laws.

2. Members of the House of Representatives and Senate _____ new laws.

3. Judges work in the courts as part of the _____ branch.

4. The United States is a _____ because citizens elect leaders.

5. An _____ is a law that has been added to the Constitution.

omit	sovereignty	representatives	federalism	define

6. States can pass traffic laws and the federal government can print money under the system called _____.

7. Citizens elect _____ who will represent them in Congress.

8. The Constitution has _____ over all other laws of the United States.

9. We can _____ "constitution" as a set of laws that govern a nation.

10. It is a mistake to _____ the sugar when baking a cake.

Name _____ Date _____

Word Challenge: Definitions

Draw a line through each incorrect definition below. Then rewrite each incorrect definition. If a definition is correct, write a sentence using the new word. The first one has been done for you.

1. A **republic** is a nation without a king or queen. _Yes. A republic is a nation that_ _has a prime minister or president as its leader._

2. **Omit** means to leave something out. _____

   _____

3. **Federalism** means that state and federal governments share power. _____

   _____

4. **Sovereignty** means that a nation can be a colony of another country. _____

   _____

Word Challenge: What's Your Answer?

Read each question and write an answer on the line. Answer the questions with complete sentences. The first one has been done for you.

1. Why would the Constitution need an **amendment**? _Certain rights_ _were left out of the original Constitution._

2. What would a person do as a **representative** in Congress? _____

   _____

3. What do you do when you **define** words? _____

   _____

4. What would you do if you worked in the **executive** branch? _____

   _____

Name _____ Date _____

Analogies

Use a word from the box to finish each sentence. Write the word on the line.

| legislate | omit | judicial | define |

1. Execute is to carry out laws as _____ is to pass laws.

2. Include is to take in as _____ is to leave out.

3. Build is to toolbox as _____ is to dictionary.

4. Executive branch is to President as _____ branch is to Chief Justice.

Word Study: The Suffix *-ism*

When you add the suffix *-ism* to an adjective like *regional,* it does two things.
- It changes the adjective to a noun: *regionalism*.
- It changes the meaning of the word. The word now refers to something that belongs to a certain region.

regional (adj.) having to do with a certain area
regionalism (n.) something that belongs to a certain region

A. Complete the chart. Use a dictionary to check your spelling and definitions.

	+ *-ism*	Definition
1. **federal**		
2. **colonial**		
3. **agricultural**		
4. **loyal**		

B. Use a word from the chart to finish each sentence.

1. The soldier who fought on the side of the government showed _____.

2. A country that wants to build colonies is interested in _____.

Name _____   Date _____

The Language of Testing

How would you answer a question like this on a test?

Identify the branch of government that contains two houses of Congress.

    Ⓐ judicial branch
    Ⓑ executive branch
    Ⓒ legislative branch
    Ⓓ colonial branch

Tip

The word *identify* means *to point out* or *name*. In a test question, it means that you need to choose or pick the correct answer.

Test Strategy: If you see a question that uses the word *identify*, rewrite it using the words *pick* or *choose*.

1. How could you say the question above in a different way?

    _____

    _____

Try the strategy again by asking these questions in a different way.

2. Which of these was not a goal when the Constitution was written?

    Ⓐ to protect the sovereignty of the United States
    Ⓑ to create a republic
    Ⓒ to create a Parliament
    Ⓓ to create three branches of government

3. Which of these people is part of the executive branch?

    Ⓐ senators
    Ⓑ judges
    Ⓒ the President
    Ⓓ representatives

Lesson 7: The Constitution and the Bill of Rights
Vocabulary: American History, SV 9781419035012

Name _____ Date _____

On Your Own

Answer the questions.

1. Why might someone make an **amendment**? _____
   _____

2. What makes a **democracy** different from other kinds of government? _____
   _____

3. What should someone in an **executive** job be good at? _____
   _____

4. What are some things that states control under **federalism**? _____
   _____

5. What does someone in a **judicial** job do? _____
   _____

6. If you were a leader, what would you **legislate**? _____
   _____

7. Who would you like to be your **representative** to talk to your principal? Why? _____
   _____

8. What are some features of a **republic**? _____
   _____

9. Why would a country want **sovereignty**? _____
   _____

Write On!

You are on a constitutional committee in a newly developed country. What type of government do you want to create? On another sheet of paper, write a summary of at least four of the laws and policies you want to include in the new constitution. Use four or more words from the lesson correctly in your summary.

amendment	democracy	judicial	sovereignty	republic	
executive	federalism	legislate	representative	define	omit

Name _____ Date _____

Lesson 7 Assessment

Read the sentences. Look for the best word or phrase to complete each sentence. Fill in the circle for the answer you choose. The first one has been done for you.

1. John is a member of his state's House of Representatives. John takes part in _____ new laws.
   - (A) interpreting
   - (B) executing
   - (C) omitting
   - (D) legislating

2. Each state is in charge of business that takes place within its borders. This is an example of _____.
   - (A) democracy
   - (B) federalism
   - (C) sovereignty
   - (D) legislation

3. Penny wants to change a law in the Constitution. She wants to propose _____.
   - (A) an amendment
   - (B) a democracy
   - (C) a republic
   - (D) a sovereignty

4. Rosario doesn't want to tell her mother about getting in trouble at camp. She wants to _____ that part of the story.
   - (A) legislate
   - (B) omit
   - (C) define
   - (D) confirm

5. Elena works in the White House. She works for the _____.
   - (A) federalist branch
   - (B) judicial branch
   - (C) executive branch
   - (D) legislative branch

6. In ancient Athens, all male citizens voted for new laws and leaders. The government of Athens was _____.
   - (A) a sovereignty
   - (B) a democracy
   - (C) a representative
   - (D) an amendment

7. A group of senators represented the people of ancient Rome. Rome was a _____.
   - (A) republic
   - (B) sovereignty
   - (C) federalism
   - (D) mercantilism

8. Beth told Enrique what the word *sovereignty* means. She _____ it for him.
   - (A) indicated
   - (B) debated
   - (C) defined
   - (D) omitted

9. Mario's mother is a municipal court judge. She works for the _____ branch.
   - (A) federal
   - (B) legislative
   - (C) executive
   - (D) judicial

10. The United States has the power to control the government here. The country has _____.
    - (A) federalism
    - (B) sovereignty
    - (C) democracy
    - (D) republic

Growth of the New Nation

Read the first passage below. Think about the meaning of the new words printed in **bold**. Underline any definitions in the text that might help you figure out what the new words mean. The first one has been done for you.

The United States Expands

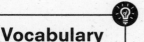

Vocabulary Strategy

Look for definitions in the text to help you understand the meanings of new words.

After the American Revolution, the United States was made up of thirteen states along the Atlantic Ocean and all of the land to the east of the Mississippi River. <u>The unsettled land between the states and the Mississippi River was called the</u> **frontier**. Soon after the American Revolution ended, many Americans began to settle the frontier. They were called **pioneers** because they were the first to move out of the colonies and into new lands. They cleared forests and built farms and cabins.

American **expansion**, or growth, angered the Native Americans who lived on the frontier. They feared that the pioneers would take away their land.

In 1830, Congress passed a law called the Indian **Removal** Act, which forced Native Americans who lived east of the Mississippi River to move to land that was west of the river. The removal of 100,000 Native Americans during the 1830s and 1840s has been **described** as unfair and cruel.

New American History Words

expansion

   noun   the act of growing larger

frontier

   noun   the outer edge of settled land

pioneer

   noun   one of the first people of a group to settle in an area or do something

   verb   to be one of the first people to do something

removal

   noun   the act of taking or moving away

Name _____ Date _____

Now read the passage below and practice the strategy again. Underline any definitions in the passage that can help you figure out what the new words in **bold** mean.

A Changing Nation

After the United States bought the Louisiana Purchase from France in 1803, it owned a huge **territory**, or land, that was west of the Mississippi River. President Thomas Jefferson wanted information about the Louisiana Territory, so he sent an **expedition**, or group of explorers, to explore it. Meriwether Lewis and William Clark led the expedition of about forty men across the territory. As they traveled, Lewis and Clark kept journals and **illustrated** them with pictures of the plants and animals they found.

In 1823, President James Monroe wrote a document called the Monroe Doctrine.

This doctrine, a document which explained his ideas, stated that Europeans could never rule colonies in America again. The United States would stay out of Europe's problems as well.

Americans in different states wanted easier ways to trade with each other. So they built **canals**, or artificial waterways, for shipping goods from one place to another. The famous Erie Canal helped New York City become the nation's busiest port.

More New American History Words

canal

noun   an artificial waterway

expedition

noun   a group that makes a trip for a specific reason, or a journey of exploration

territory

noun   land that a nation controls

A **pioneer**'s work is never done!

Other Useful Words

describe

verb   to tell what something is like

illustrate

verb   to draw pictures for a book, to explain, or to show

Apply the Strategy

Look at a chapter in your textbook that your teacher identifies. Use definitions in the text to help you figure out the meaning of any new words you find.

Name _____ Date _____

 Find the Word

Write a word from the box next to each clue. Then write the word made by the boxed letters to answer the question below. One word will be used twice.

pioneer	expedition	canal	illustrate	frontier
describe	removal	territory	expansion	

1. to draw a picture of something   ___ ___ ___ ___ ___ ___ ___ ___ ☐

2. a journey of exploration   ___ ☐ ___ ___ ___ ___ ___ ___ ___

3. growth   ___ ___ ☐ ___ ___ ___ ___ ___

4. taking away   ___ ___ ☐ ___ ___ ___ ___

5. to tell what something is like   ☐ ___ ___ ___ ___ ___ ___

6. show or explain   ☐ ___ ___ ___ ___ ___ ___ ___ ___

7. land controlled by a nation   ☐ ___ ___ ___ ___ ___ ___

8. the first to settle an area   ___ ☐ ___ ___ ___ ___ ___

9. unsettled land   ___ ___ ☐ ___ ___ ___ ___ ___

10. waterway   ___ ___ ☐ ___ ___

What did Lewis and Clark lead? An ___ ___ ___ ___ ___ ___ ___ ___ ___ ___ ___

Name _____ Date _____

Word Challenge: Word Association

Read the groups of words below. Write the word from the lesson that goes best with each group. The first one has been done for you.

1. _____*pioneers*_____ new settlers, lead the way

2. _____ team, journey, voyage

3. _____ land, country, control

4. _____ growing larger, spreading out

5. _____ draw pictures, explain

Word Challenge: Would You Rather . . .

Read the questions below. Think of a response and write it on the line. Explain your answers. The first one has been done for you.

1. Would you rather help with garbage **removal** or garbage **expansion**? _____*I'd*_____ *rather help with the garbage removal, because there's already too much garbage.*

2. Would you rather **describe** your favorite car in a paragraph or **illustrate** it?

   _____

3. Would you rather be a **pioneer** or be part of an **expedition**? _____

   _____

4. Would you rather live on the **frontier** or in a **territory**? _____

   _____

Name _____ Date _____

Extend the Meaning

Write the letter of the word or phrase that best completes each sentence.

1. To **describe** a painting, you would talk about _____.

   a. colonies and settlements

   b. Native American clothing

   c. colors, shapes, and pictures

2. You might want to **illustrate** _____.

   a. a road map

   b. a story book

   c. a charter

3. You might wish to join an **expedition** to _____.

   a. swim in a hotel pool

   b. climb a very tall mountain

   c. read a library book

4. Expansion of the United States was helped by the _____.

   a. writing of the Constitution

   b. mercenary soldiers

   c. Louisiana Purchase

Word Study: The Root *mov*

Mov is the root in the words *movie* and *removal*. The root *mov* means "move."

You can make many *mov* words by adding:
• prefixes like *re-*, *un-*, and *im-*
• suffixes like *-ment*, *-able*, and *-ability*

Add the prefixes and suffixes below to the root *mov* to make new words. Write a definition for each new word. Use a dictionary to check your spelling and definitions.

Prefixes	Suffixes	Word	Definition
1. *re-*		remove	
2. *re-*	*-able*		
3.	*-ment*		
4. *im-*	*-able*		

Vocabulary: American History, SV 9781419035012

Name _____ Date _____

The Language of Testing

How would you answer a question like this on a test?

The Lewis and Clark expedition
was characterized by _____.

Ⓐ pioneers settling on the frontier

Ⓑ the building of the Erie Canal

Ⓒ men exploring the Louisiana Territory

Ⓓ new tariffs on American goods

Tip

The phrase *was characterized by* means you must find one answer that has information about the topic of the question.

Test Strategy: Look for an answer that has the best information for the question.

1. How could you ask the question above in a different way?

_____

_____

Try the strategy again by asking these questions in a different way.

2. The Monroe Doctrine was characterized by _____.

Ⓐ words from the Bill of Rights

Ⓑ explanation that European countries should stay out of America

Ⓒ its warning to King George

Ⓓ a plan to explore new territories

_____

_____

_____

_____

3. The Indian Removal Act was characterized by _____.

Ⓐ the forced movement of Native Americans to land west of the Mississippi

Ⓑ new leadership

Ⓒ a battle to win land in Florida

Ⓓ the movement of people to Canada

_____

_____

_____

_____

Vocabulary: American History, SV 9781419035012

Name _____ Date _____

 On Your Own

Answer the questions.

1. What can a **canal** be used for? _____

   _____

2. What do you think is the next area for **expansion**? _____

   _____

3. Where would you like to go on an **expedition**? _____

   _____

4. What do you think the **frontier** was like? _____

   _____

5. Who is a modern **pioneer**? _____

   _____

6. Why were certain groups chosen for **removal** from the land? _____

   _____

7. What places do you consider your **territory**? _____

   _____

 Write On!

You are a member of the Lewis and Clark expedition exploring the Louisiana Territory. On another sheet of paper, write a journal entry about one day of the expedition. Be sure to include descriptions of what you see and hear as you walk across the frontier. Use four or more words from the lesson correctly in your journal entry.

frontier	pioneer	expansion	removal	expedition
territory	canal	describe	illustrate	

Name _____ Date _____

Lesson 8 Assessment

Read the sentences. Look for the best word to complete the sentence. Fill in the circle for the answer you choose. The first one has been done for you.

1. A canal _____.
   - (A) cannot be used by boats
   - (B) is formed by an iceberg
   - (C) is filled with mud
   - (D) is artificially made

2. The Louisiana Territory was _____.
   - (A) originally owned by Russia
   - (B) part of the first thirteen colonies
   - (C) west of the Mississippi River
   - (D) land sold by the United States to France

3. A writer would most likely want to illustrate _____.
   - (A) a children's book
   - (B) a dictionary
   - (C) a book on politics
   - (D) a collection of American literature

4. The pioneers _____.
   - (A) converted all Native Americans to Christianity
   - (B) revolted against the American government
   - (C) were the first people to settle in an unknown area
   - (D) wanted to move back to England

5. The Lewis and Clark expedition explored _____.
   - (A) northern Canada
   - (B) land west of the Mississippi River
   - (C) Alaska
   - (D) Hawaii

6. Thomas Jefferson's support of the Lewis and Clark expedition illustrated that he _____.
   - (A) did not trust France
   - (B) thought the U.S. should stay small
   - (C) did not want Native Americans to lose their land
   - (D) believed in westward expansion

7. American expansion _____.
   - (A) was not very popular
   - (B) led to the loss of several states
   - (C) angered the Native Americans
   - (D) caused a war with the French

8. The Indian Removal Act _____.
   - (A) forced Native Americans to move west of the Mississippi River
   - (B) allowed Native Americans to stay on their homeland
   - (C) gave the U.S. permission to take over the Louisiana Territory
   - (D) did not affect many Native Americans

9. People who lived on the frontier _____.
   - (A) had plenty of places to shop
   - (B) were safe from animal attacks
   - (C) had to build houses and hunt for food
   - (D) didn't work very hard

10. Many people describe the Indian Removal Act of 1830 as _____.
    - (A) an obstacle to American expansion
    - (B) unfair and cruel
    - (C) not that important in U.S. history
    - (D) necessary for the Indians' safety

Lesson 9

The Civil War and Reconstruction

Read the passage below. Think about the meaning of the new words printed in **bold**. Circle familiar words in some of the new words that might help you figure out their meaning. The first one has been done for you.

The United States Is Divided

Vocabulary Strategy

Use words you know to help unlock the meaning of unfamiliar words in the same family. For example, *construct* can help you unlock the meaning of *reconstruct* and *reconstruction*.

Slaves were first brought from Africa to work in the American colonies in the 1600s. In the South, people depended on (slavery) to run their huge cotton, sugar, and tobacco plantations. But many people in the North thought slavery was wrong. They wanted to abolish, or end, slavery. Anger about the **abolition** of slavery grew between the North and South.

In 1861, Abraham Lincoln was elected President. The South believed Lincoln would end slavery. As a result, eleven Southern states decided to **secede**, or stop being part of the United States. They formed their own country called the Confederate States of America, or the **Confederacy**. Some of the states in the Confederacy were Texas, Virginia, Georgia, and Florida. Their names can be **abbreviated** as TX, VA, GA, and FL.

In 1861, the United States and the Confederacy began to fight. This war is called the Civil War. Thousands of Americans were killed during the four years of this terrible war.

New American History Words

abolition

noun   the act of ending something, especially slavery

confederacy

noun   a group of states or people with the same goals, or the group of states that broke away from the United States in 1860–1861

secede

verb   to leave a group

slavery

noun   the practice of owning people as property

Name _____ Date _____

Now read the passage below and practice the vocabulary strategy again. Underline familiar words that are found in larger, unfamiliar words.

After the Civil War

President Lincoln issued the **Emancipation** Proclamation in 1863. This document said slaves in the Confederacy were free. However, slaves really received emancipation, or freedom, after the Civil War ended in 1865. In that year the Thirteenth Amendment ended slavery forever.

After the Confederacy surrendered, the North and South were one nation again. Much of the South had to be rebuilt after the war, however. The years after the Civil War were called **Reconstruction**. This name refers to the rebuilding of the South.

The events of Reconstruction can be **summarized**, or stated briefly, in a few sentences. Soldiers were sent to control the South. Cities, railroads, and farms were rebuilt. In 1872, Congress gave **amnesty**, or the government's forgiveness, to most people in the South.

The North and the South **compromised** about when the army should leave the South. The Compromise of 1877 said the army would leave and the Southern states would rejoin the United States. In return, African Americans in the South would be allowed to vote.

More New American History Words

amnesty

  noun government forgiveness of crimes

compromise

  verb to give up something to end an argument

  noun an agreement reached when both sides give up something they want to solve an argument

emancipation

  noun freedom from something, especially slavery

reconstruction

  noun a period of rebuilding, or the rebuilding of the South after the Civil War

Other Useful Words

abbreviate

  verb to shorten

summarize

  verb to explain briefly by telling the most important ideas

Apply the Strategy

Look at a chapter in your textbook that your teacher identifies. Use familiar words to help you unlock the meaning of unfamiliar words.

Name _____ Date _____

Finish the Paragraphs

Use the words in bold to finish each paragraph below. Write the words in the blanks. One word in each box will not be used.

slavery	**staple**	**Confederacy**	**seceded**	**abolition**

Many people in the North thought _____ was wrong. Therefore,

1.

they worked for the _____ of slavery. In the South, people

2.

believed they needed slaves for their plantations. In 1861, eleven southern states left the

United States when they _____. They started a country called the

3.

Confederate States of America. The abbreviated name was the _____.

4.

amnesty	**revolution**	**emancipation**	**Reconstruction**	**compromised**

The period in which Americans rebuilt the South after the Civil War was called

_____. The _____ of all slaves gave them their

5. 6.

freedom. Most people who served the Confederacy were forgiven by the United States

government and given _____. Reconstruction ended in 1877 when

7.

the North and South _____ and agreed to let the South rejoin the

8.

United States if African Americans were allowed to vote.

Name _____ Date _____

Word Challenge: Think About It

Write a sentence to answer each question. The first one has been done for you.

1. Many people in the North worked for the **abolition** of slavery. How do you think they felt about slavery? _They wanted slavery to end._

2. The South **seceded** from the United States in 1861. How do you think the South felt about the United States? _____ _____

3. The **emancipation** of slaves took place after the Civil War. How do you think slaves felt about emancipation? _____ _____

4. Sumita **summarizes** textbook chapters after reading them. How do you think summarizing helps Sumita? _____ _____

Word Challenge: What's Your Answer?

Read each question and write an answer on the line. Answer the questions in complete sentences. The first one has been done for you.

1. Why would you and your friend agree to a **compromise**? _We would_ _agree to a compromise to end an argument._

2. What would you have done during **Reconstruction**? _____ _____

3. Why would you oppose **slavery**? _____ _____

4. What kind of words do you **abbreviate**? _____ _____

Vocabulary: American History, SV 9781419035012

Name _____   Date _____

Synonyms or Antonyms

Look at each group of words below. Circle two words in each group that are synonyms or the two words that are antonyms. Then write *synonyms* or *antonyms* on the line.

1. emancipation   freedom

   abbreviate   reconstruction

   _____

2. summarize   constitution

   lengthen   judge

   _____

3. compromise   empire

   slavery   agreement

   _____

4. reconstruction   export

   agriculture   rebuilding

   _____

Word Study: The Prefix *re-*

The prefix *re-* means "again" or "repeat." It is often used with verbs, such as *write*. In some cases the new word can be both a noun and a verb.

rewrite (v.) to write something again
rewrite (n.) something that has been written again

A. Decide whether the word is a noun, a verb, or both. Write a definition for each.

	Noun, Verb, or Both?	Definition
1. **reorganize**		
2. **reorder**		
3. **reconstruct**		

B. Write a word from the chart that describes what is happening in the sentence.

1. _____ We need to order more pizzas for the party.

2. _____ The class organized its class library again.

Lesson 9: The Civil War and Reconstruction
Vocabulary: American History, SV 9781419035012

Name _____   Date _____

The Language of Testing

How do you answer a question like this on a test?

Which of the following is correct?

Ⓐ Americans own slaves today.
Ⓑ People were elected to be slaves.
Ⓒ Slaves did not have freedom.
Ⓓ Most slaves lived in the North.

Tip

The phrase *which of the following* means that you need to choose one of the answers (A, B, C, or D) to answer the question.

Test Strategy: Always read the whole question and the answers first. If the question has the phrase *which of the following* in it, ask the question in a different way. Start your question with *what*, *who*, or *where*.

1. How would you write the question above in a different way?

_____

_____

Try the strategy again by asking these questions in a different way.

2. Which of the following served as President during the Civil War?

Ⓐ Herbert Hoover
Ⓑ Abraham Lincoln
Ⓒ George Washington
Ⓓ George Bush

3. Which of the following fought against the United States during the Civil War?

Ⓐ China
Ⓑ Confederacy
Ⓒ Spain
Ⓓ Britain

_____   _____

_____   _____

_____   _____

_____   _____

_____   _____

Lesson 9: The Civil War and Reconstruction
Vocabulary: American History, SV 9781419035012

Name _____ Date _____

 On Your Own

Answer the questions.

1. What verb is the word *abolition* related to? _____

_____

2. When have you been shown **amnesty**? _____

_____

3. Describe a time you had to **compromise** with someone. _____

_____

4. What are some features of a **confederacy**? _____

_____

5. What are some kinds of **emancipation**? _____

_____

6. What happened during **Reconstruction**? _____

_____

7. Why might a state want to **secede**? _____

_____

8. How did **slavery** end in the United States? _____

_____

 Write On!

You are a Northerner in the time just before the Civil War. You are working for the abolition of slavery and are trying to convince others to help you. On another sheet of paper, write a short speech in which you explain your feelings about slavery and what you are doing to stop it. Use four or more words from the lesson correctly in your speech.

| confederacy | abolition | abbreviate | slavery | emancipation |
| reconstruction | amnesty | compromise | secede | summarize |

Name _____ Date _____

Lesson 9 Assessment

Read the sentences. Look for the best word or phrase to complete each sentence. Fill in the circle for the answer you choose. The first one has been done for you.

1. On December 20, 1860, South Carolina _____ from the United States.
   - (A) seceded
   - (B) exported
   - (C) abbreviated
   - (D) repealed

2. While Missouri and Kentucky technically remained part of the United States, several sects within them became part of the _____.
   - (A) enterprise
   - (B) revolution
   - (C) reconstruction
   - (D) Confederacy

3. The success of many cotton plantations depended on _____.
   - (A) abolition
   - (B) slavery
   - (C) emancipation
   - (D) secession

4. In 1868, President Andrew Johnson granted _____ to the former Confederate states.
   - (A) emancipation
   - (B) sovereignty
   - (C) amnesty
   - (D) sedition

5. People who took part in the Underground Railroad were working for the _____ of slavery.
   - (A) emancipation
   - (B) abolition
   - (C) reconstruction
   - (D) expansion

6. The Senate and House of Representatives were created as part of a _____ between large and small states over representation in Congress.
   - (A) treaty
   - (B) amnesty
   - (C) enterprise
   - (D) compromise

7. During _____, many African Americans were allowed to vote for the first time.
   - (A) Reconstruction
   - (B) emancipation
   - (C) mercantilism
   - (D) abolition

8. You can _____ Abraham Lincoln's Emancipation Proclamation as a grant of freedom for all slaves.
   - (A) abbreviate
   - (B) compromise
   - (C) summarize
   - (D) secede

9. You can _____ the Federal Bureau of Investigation as the FBI.
   - (A) portray
   - (B) abbreviate
   - (C) summarize
   - (D) compromise

10. One of the most important outcomes of the Civil War was the _____ of the slaves.
   - (A) abolition
   - (B) reconstruction
   - (C) confederacy
   - (D) emancipation

Name _____   Date _____

Growth of American Industries

Read the passage below. Decide if each new word printed in **bold** is a noun or a verb. Write *noun* or *verb* near each word. Then use that information with other clues in the text to figure out what the new word means. The first one has been done for you.

The First Industrial Revolution

noun

The Industrial Revolution began in America in 1790. It was a peaceful change from making goods by hand to **manufacturing**, or making goods by machines.

In 1790, machines that made **textiles**, or cloth, were built in America. The new machines were too large to be used at home, so **entrepreneurs** built factories. The location of rivers was one **factor** that helped entrepreneurs decide where to build factories. Factory owners used rivers to power the machines. They also used rivers to ship textiles to other places.

Factory owners wanted to produce large amounts of goods quickly. Producing large amounts of a product at a time is known as mass production. An important step in mass production was to develop parts that could work in many products. These parts were called **interchangeable** parts. After Americans learned to make interchangeable parts, they could make factory goods more quickly.

Interchangeable parts were first used to make guns for the army. Each gun was the same, so parts from one gun could be used to repair another. During the 1800s, America became a leader in manufacturing. This was largely the result of mass production and interchangeable parts.

Vocabulary Strategy

Identify if a new word is used as a noun or a verb. Then use that information with other clues in the text to figure out what the new word means.

New American History Words

entrepreneur

noun   a person who starts and runs a business

interchangeable

adjective   something that can be used in place of something else

manufacturing

noun   the process of making goods in a factory

verb   making goods in a factory

textiles

noun   cloth

Now read the passage below and practice the vocabulary strategy again. Write *noun* or *verb* above each new word printed in **bold**.

The Growth of Big Business

During the late 1800s, John D. Rockefeller became very rich by controlling America's oil business. At first Rockefeller owned just one oil company. He used his **capital**, or money he had earned from that business, to buy most of the nation's oil companies.

Rockefeller believed in a system called **capitalism**. This means the government allows people to own and control businesses.

In the late 1800s, most large businesses were organized as **corporations**. A corporation is a company that is often controlled by a group of people called a board of directors.

After Rockefeller gained control of many oil corporations, he formed a **trust**. A trust is a group of corporations that are controlled by one board of directors. Rockefeller could control the price of America's oil because he controlled the oil trust.

Many Americans said Rockefeller had too much control of the oil industry. They **concluded**, or decided, that laws were needed to control trusts and businesses. Congress passed new laws to control trusts.

More New American History Words

capital

noun   money or property used to start and run a business

capitalism

noun   a system in which the people of a country own businesses and earn profits

corporation

noun   a business or company

trust

noun   a group of corporations controlled by one organization

verb   to believe to be honest or dependable

"Why do people think I'm rich? I own only one **trust**."

Other Useful Words

conclude

verb   to make a decision based on known facts

factor

noun   something that affects a decision, an event, or what a person does

Apply the Strategy

Look at a chapter in your textbook that your teacher identifies. Identify the parts of speech of new words to help you figure out their meanings.

Name _____   Date _____

 Matching

Finish the sentences in Group A with words from Group B. Write the letter of the word on the line.

Group A

1. We counted all our money, and we _____ that we had enough to host a party.

2. Americans can own businesses because our country supports _____.

3. Our telephones were made with _____ parts.

4. I was known as an _____ when I started a successful business.

5. Many corporations were controlled by one _____.

Group B

A. capitalism

B. interchangeable

C. concluded

D. trust

E. entrepreneur

Group A

6. We need money, or _____, to start a business.

7. Japanese companies are _____ fine cars.

8. Most clothing is made from _____.

9. Most department stores are run as _____.

10. The location of rivers was a _____ when deciding where to build factories.

Group B

F. corporations

G. manufacturing

H. factor

I. capital

J. textiles

Lesson 10: Growth of American Industries
Vocabulary: American History, SV 9781419035012

Name _____ Date _____

Word Challenge: Would You Rather . . .

Read the statements below. Think of a response and write it on the line. Explain your answers. The first one has been done for you.

1. Would you rather be an **entrepreneur** or work for a **corporation**? _____ *I would*

   rather be an entrepreneur because I want to be my own boss.

2. Would you rather own a lot of **capital** or own a **trust**? _____

   _____

3. Would you rather live under **capitalism** or another system? _____

   _____

4. Would you rather **conclude** something based on facts or **factors**? _____

   _____

Word Challenge: Finish the Idea

Read the incomplete sentences below. Write an ending for each. The first one has been done for you.

1. People might want to live in a country that allows **capitalism** because

   capitalism allows people to own their own businesses.

2. One **factor** for a good party is _____

3. I want my business to be a **corporation** because _____

   _____

4. I **concluded** that we had a good time on vacation because _____

   _____

Lesson 10: Growth of American Industries
Vocabulary: American History, SV 9781419035012

Name _____ Date _____

Extend the Meaning

Write the letter of the word or phrase that best completes each sentence.

1. You would use **textiles** to _____.
   a. bake a cake
   b. make a coat
   c. write a letter

2. **Manufacturing** could create _____.
   a. oranges
   b. computers
   c. flowers

3. You would probably find **interchangeable** parts on a _____.
   a. car
   b. apple
   c. banana

4. An **entrepreneur** might _____.
   a. shop in a department store
   b. study in college
   c. start a new supermarket

Word Study: The Suffix -able

When you add the suffix -able to a verb like debate, two things happen.
   • The word becomes an adjective: debatable.
   • The word now means "able to be debated."

Sometimes when a word ends with an e, you must drop the e before adding -able.

changeable (adj.) can be changed
washable (adj.) can be washed

A. Add the suffix -able to the words below and write a definition for each new word. Use a dictionary to check your spelling and definitions.

	+ -able	Definition
1. **predict**		
2. **describe**		
3. **expand**		
4. **confirm**		

B. Write sentences for two of the -able words from the chart.

1. _____

2. _____

82

Name _____ Date _____

The Language of Testing

How would you answer a question like this on a test?

What conclusion can be drawn about manufacturing textiles?

    Ⓐ The work should be done by hand.

    Ⓑ It is faster to make textiles by machine.

    Ⓒ People do not need textiles.

    Ⓓ All textiles are ugly.

Tip

When *what conclusion can be drawn* is used in a question, it means "what happened?" or "why did this happen?" You must choose the best possible reason from the choices.

Test Strategy: If the question has the phrase *what conclusion can be drawn* in it, rewrite it to ask *what happened*, or *why did this happen?*

1. How could you say the question above in a different way?

_____

_____

Try the strategy again by asking these questions in a different way.

2. John D. Rockefeller became rich from his oil business. What conclusion can be drawn about Rockefeller?

    Ⓐ Rockefeller had many friends.

    Ⓑ Rockefeller controlled most of America's oil.

    Ⓒ Rockefeller enjoyed traveling.

    Ⓓ Rockefeller's family was poor.

_____

_____

_____

_____

3. Factories were built near rivers. What conclusion can be drawn from this?

    Ⓐ Rivers were used to ship goods.

    Ⓑ Workers swam in the rivers.

    Ⓒ People fished in the rivers.

    Ⓓ River water was used to wash textiles.

_____

_____

_____

_____

Lesson 10: Growth of American Industries
Vocabulary: American History, SV 9781419035012

Name _____ Date _____

Answer the questions.

1. What do you need **capital** for? _____
   _____

2. What are some features of **capitalism**? _____
   _____

3. Would you choose to work for a **corporation**? Why? _____
   _____

4. If you were an **entrepeneur**, what type of business would you have? ____
   _____

5. What are some things that are **interchangeable**? _____
   _____

6. List one good thing and one bad thing about **manufacturing**. _____
   _____

7. What things are made out of **textiles**? _____
   _____

8. How are **trusts** bad for an economy? _____
   _____

Write On!

You are an entrepreneur who is trying to raise capital for a business you wish to start. On another sheet of paper, write a letter to a potential investor (someone who could loan you money) and explain the idea for your business and why you think it will be successful. Use four or more words from the lesson correctly in your letter.

manufacturing interchangeable	textiles conclude	entrepreneur corporation	capitalism capital	trust factor

Lesson 10 Assessment

Read the sentences. Look for the best word or phrase to complete each sentence. Fill in the circle for the answer you choose. The first one has been done for you.

1. Maria's mechanic replaced her brakes. The brakes are an example of _____.
   Ⓐ manufacturing
   Ⓑ textiles
   Ⓒ interchangeable parts
   Ⓓ capital

2. Eric decided that he would stay home from school because he had a sore throat. Eric came to a _____.
   Ⓐ factor
   Ⓑ conclusion
   Ⓒ sedition
   Ⓓ contrast

3. Julio has decided he wants to start a music store. He is a(n) _____.
   Ⓐ entrepreneur
   Ⓑ conclusion
   Ⓒ trust
   Ⓓ manufacturer

4. Manny's motorcycle was made in a factory. Manny's motorcycle is a product of _____.
   Ⓐ compromise
   Ⓑ manufacturing
   Ⓒ mercantilism
   Ⓓ agriculture

5. Keisha saw a dog foaming at the mouth and twitching. She _____ that the dog had rabies.
   Ⓐ concluded
   Ⓑ compromised
   Ⓒ factored
   Ⓓ interchanged

6. MegaCompuComp raises money by selling shares of stock. MegaCompuComp is an example of a _____.
   Ⓐ textile
   Ⓑ proprietor
   Ⓒ trust
   Ⓓ corporation

7. Silk, cotton, and linen are examples of _____.
   Ⓐ corporations
   Ⓑ textiles
   Ⓒ interchangeable parts
   Ⓓ trusts

8. Carla needs money so she can start a craft store. She needs to raise some _____.
   Ⓐ capital
   Ⓑ factors
   Ⓒ conclusions
   Ⓓ corporations

9. U.S. Steel Corporation owned a large number of other steel companies. The government accused U.S. Steel of forming a(n) _____.
   Ⓐ assembly
   Ⓑ empire
   Ⓒ corporation
   Ⓓ trust

10. The fall of the U.S.S.R. in 1991 led to the development of businesses by individuals. This new economy is an example of _____.
    Ⓐ mercantilism
    Ⓑ reconstruction
    Ⓒ capitalism
    Ⓓ manufacturing

Lesson 11

Name _____ Date _____

Social Issues and Reform

Read the passage below. Think about the meanings of the new words printed in **bold**. Underline any examples or descriptions you find that might help you figure out the meaning of new words. Draw an arrow from the examples and descriptions to the word each describes. The first one has been done for you.

A Changing Nation

At the end of the 1800s, a group of people called **progressives** wanted to help the nation make progress and solve problems in American life.

The United States was changing in the late 1800s because of **immigration**, or the movement of people from many other countries into the country. Millions of poor immigrants started new lives in the United States. Some people called **nativists** were against immigration into the United States. They succeeded in having Congress pass laws limiting immigration.

By the late 1800s, the nation had many factories. Men, women, and children worked hard as factory workers, but they earned very little money. A number of people **analyzed**, or studied, the problems of poor workers. Some people thought that **socialism** might solve their problems. Under socialism, the government owns and controls all businesses. Capitalism won out, however. Progressives turned to other ideas to solve America's problems.

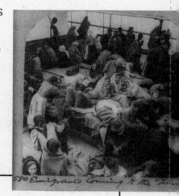

Vocabulary Strategy

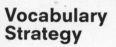

Use examples and descriptions to help you figure out the meaning of new words. Look for clues such as *for example*, *like*, or *such as*. Look for pictures that might show you what a new word means, too.

New American History Words

immigration

noun   the act of moving into a new country

nativist

noun   someone who is against people from other countries moving in

progressive

noun   a person who wants to make society better

adjective   having to do with improving things in a modern way

socialism

noun   a system in which the government controls businesses and industries and all people are treated equally

Name _____ Date _____

Now read the passages below and practice the strategy again. Underline examples or descriptions in the passage. Draw arrows from the examples and descriptions to the new word each describes.

 # Improving America

Another way the progressives tried to improve American life was through **conservation**, or protecting the land, air, and water. President Teddy Roosevelt was a progressive. He worked with Congress to pass laws that created many national parks.

Teddy Roosevelt disliked trusts like the one that John D. Rockefeller controlled. Roosevelt believed they had too much control over American businesses. He acted on, or **responded** to, this problem by working with Congress. Laws were passed to break trusts up into smaller companies.

Segregation, the separation of people by race, was also a problem. In the South, African Americans had to use separate schools, parks, hospitals, and beaches. Some people began working for **integration**, allowing all races to use the same places.

Since the United States had first become a nation, women were not allowed to vote. But women across America worked hard to win **suffrage**, the right to vote. In 1920, the Nineteenth Amendment gave all women in the United States the right to vote.

 ## More New American History Words

conservation
> *noun*   saving and protecting the air, land, water, and resources

integration
> *noun*   to join together people of different races

segregation
> *noun*   the act of separating people by race

suffrage
> *noun*   the right to vote

Many people suffered for my **suffrage**. That's why I vote!

 ## Apply the Strategy

Look at a chapter in your textbook that your teacher identifies. Use examples, descriptions, and pictures in the text to help you figure out the meaning of any new words you find. You might also draw pictures to help you remember what new words mean.

 ## Other Useful Words

analyze
> *verb*   to study or think about something carefully in order to understand it

respond
> *verb*   to do or say something about what was done or said

Name _____   Date _____

 Finish the Sentence

Use a word from the box to finish each sentence. Write the correct word on the line.

nativists	analyzed	socialism	progressives	immigration

1. During a period of _____, millions of people moved to America from Europe.

2. Americans called _____ did not want immigrants to come to America.

3. The economic system in which the government owns and controls industries and businesses is _____.

4. People who worked to improve society were _____.

5. In order to write a book report, I _____ the book carefully.

responded	suffrage	conservation	integration	segregation

6. Eric received a party invitation and _____ by saying he would be there.

7. People who protect the nation's air, land, and water care about _____.

8. Today, American men and women vote in elections because they all have

_____.

9. At one time, African Americans had to use separate parks because of

_____.

10. Students of all ethnicities now go to school together because of _____.

Name _____ Date _____

Word Challenge: What's Your Answer?

Read each question and write an answer on the line. Answer the questions in complete sentences. The first one has been done for you.

1. What kind of work would you do for **conservation**? _I would plant trees for_

conservation.

2. How would you **respond** if you won an award? _____

_____

3. What might you say to a **nativist**? _____

_____

4. What kind of problem would you need to **analyze**? _____

_____

Word Challenge: Word Associations

Read the group of words below. Write the word from the lesson that goes best with each group. The first one has been done for you.

1. ___progressive___ improve society, use new ideas

2. _____ equal treatment for all, government controls businesses

3. _____ separation by race, inequal treatment

4. _____ protect land and water, save resources

5. _____ no immigrants, Americans only

Name _____ Date _____

Finish the Idea

Finish each idea to make a complete sentence. Write your answer on the line.

1. I would be against **segregation** because _____

_____

2. American women wanted **suffrage** because _____

_____

3. I would have worked for **integration** in the United States because _____

_____

4. I would have helped the **progressives** because _____

_____

Word Study: The Suffix *-ive*

When you add the suffix *-ive* to a word like *progress,* two things happen.
- The suffix *-ive* turns the word into an adjective: *progressive.*
- The word now means "using or being interested in new ideas."

Some *-ive* words like *progressive* can also be nouns. A few other words like this are *representative, executive,* and *objective.*

A. Add the *-ive* suffix to the words in the chart. Write your own definition of each. Use a dictionary to check your spelling and your definitions.

	+ *-ive*	Definition
1. **expense**		
2. **repulse**		
3. **attract**		

B. Use a word from the chart to finish each sentence.

1. The pretty girl is very _____.

2. The dirty restaurant was a _____ place to eat.

3. The shoes cost too much money, so they were _____.

Name _____   Date _____

The Language of Testing

What do you do when you read a question like this on a test?

Teddy Roosevelt was

most closely associated with

Ⓐ conservation
Ⓑ the American Revolution
Ⓒ the Civil War
Ⓓ Jamestown

Tip

The phrase *most closely associated with* means you need to find the answer that has the closest connection to the person, event, or thing mentioned in the question.

Test Strategy: If the question has the phrase *most closely associated with*, ask yourself which of the choices has the closest relationship to the question.

1. How could you say the question above in a different way?

_____

_____

Try the strategy again by asking these questions in a different way.

2. The period of immigration after 1870 was most closely associated with

Ⓐ the building of new schools
Ⓑ the end of slavery
Ⓒ millions of people moving to America from Europe
Ⓓ a boycott against Britain

_____

_____

_____

_____

3. The problem of segregation was most closely associated with

Ⓐ building new roads
Ⓑ the unfair treatment of African Americans
Ⓒ women voting for president
Ⓓ new factories in America

_____

_____

_____

_____

Lesson 11: Social Issues and Reform
Vocabulary: American History, SV 9781419035012

Name _____ Date _____

On Your Own

Answer the questions.

1. Why is **conservation** important? _____

   _____

2. How does **immigration** change a country? _____

   _____

3. What things can be **integrated**? _____

   _____

4. What things might a **nativist** support? _____

   _____

5. What things might a **progressive** try to change? _____

   _____

6. What are some examples of **segregation**? _____

   _____

7. What makes **socialism** different from capitalism? _____

   _____

8. Why is it important for everyone to have **suffrage**? _____

   _____

Write On!

You are a newspaper columnist and a progressive. On another sheet of paper, write a well-organized column for your paper in which you explain your beliefs and describe three or more successful actions that have been completed by your fellow progressives. Use four or more words from the lesson correctly in your column.

progressive	**immigration**	**nativist**	**socialism**	**conservation**
segregation	**integration**	**suffrage**	**analyze**	**respond**

Name _____ Date _____

Lesson 11 Assessment

Read the sentences. Look for the best word to complete each sentence. Fill in the circle for the answer you choose. The first one has been done for you.

1. A group of _____ complained that too many people were moving to the United States from other countries.
   - **(A)** nativists
   - (B) pioneers
   - (C) progressives
   - (D) representatives

2. Alice Paul fought for _____ for women by organizing large public demonstrations.
   - (A) conservation
   - (B) integration
   - (C) suffrage
   - (D) socialism

3. The police detective _____ the evidence found at the crime scene for clues.
   - (A) analyzed
   - (B) responded
   - (C) concluded
   - (D) illustrated

4. Rosa Parks fought against _____ by refusing to give up her seat on a bus to a white person.
   - (A) integration
   - (B) socialism
   - (C) segregation
   - (D) nativists

5. _____ wanted to improve conditions for workers.
   - (A) Capitalists
   - (B) Dissenters
   - (C) Nativists
   - (D) Progressives

6. My grandfather did not want to live in a country that practiced _____ because he wanted to own his own business.
   - (A) mercantilism
   - (B) socialism
   - (C) segregation
   - (D) capitalism

7. Many Americans _____ to the attacks on September 11, 2001, by flying American flags.
   - (A) analyzed
   - (B) predicted
   - (C) responded
   - (D) proposed

8. In September 1957, nine black students entered an all-white high school as part of _____.
   - (A) conservation
   - (B) immigration
   - (C) segregation
   - (D) integration

9. The Irish Potato Famine led to a rise in _____ of the Irish to America.
   - (A) conservation
   - (B) segregation
   - (C) immigration
   - (D) integration

10. Driving a hybrid car to save fuel is one way you can practice _____.
    - (A) socialism
    - (B) conservation
    - (C) suffrage
    - (D) integration

Lesson 12

Name _____ Date _____

World War I

Read the passage below. Think about the meaning of the words printed in **bold**. Circle any words ending in *-ism*. Remember that *-ism* often refers to a belief or idea. Write near the circled words what you think they mean. The first one has been done for you.

Causes of World War I

Vocabulary Strategy

Use familiar prefixes and suffixes to help you understand the meaning of new words.

In 1914, most of Europe began fighting in a war that later came to be called World War I. During this war, Britain and France fought against Germany and Austria-Hungary. Other nations joined in as the war continued.

There were three major causes of the war. First, throughout Europe, there were strong feelings of **nationalism**. Nationalism means people feel their country is the best. In Germany, nationalism made the government wish to control other nations.

strong national feeling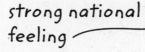

A second cause of the war was **militarism**. Militarism means the building of strong armies. Militarism made countries believe that they could win control of others with their strong armies.

A third cause was **imperialism**. Imperialism means building an empire. Nations in Europe competed for colonies in Africa and Asia.

When World War I began, the United States believed in **isolationism**. The United States did not want to be part of the problems in Europe. However, newspapers **informed** Americans about the events of the war. This changed the public's feelings about the war. In 1917, the United States entered World War I to fight alongside Britain and France.

New American History Words

imperialism

noun   a belief that a strong nation builds and controls colonies

isolationism

noun   a nation's decision to not get involved with other countries

militarism

noun   the building of a powerful military that can be used for war

nationalism

noun   strong love for one's country and feeling that it is better than others

Vocabulary: American History, SV 9781419035012

Name _____ Date _____

Now read the passage below and practice the strategy again. Circle any new words that contain familiar prefixes or suffixes that can help you figure out the meaning of new words.

The United States in World War I

In 1917, the United States began fighting against Germany and Austria-Hungary in World War I. The United States needed a large number of soldiers. The nation **mobilized**, or put together, its army. These soldiers went to Europe to fight in support of Britain and France. Some nations in Europe, such as Spain and Switzerland, were **neutral**, and did not fight during the war.

The United States helped Britain and France defeat Germany. On November 11, 1918, an **armistice** ended World War I. The world had peace. The President of the United States, Woodrow Wilson, made a peace plan called the Fourteen Points. One of his points was that people should have **self-determination**, or control over their nation. Wilson **assumed**, or believed, that his peace plan would bring real peace to the world. By 1939, however, the world would be fighting in another terrible world war.

 ## More New American History Words

armistice

noun   an agreement by enemy nations to stop fighting during a war

mobilize

verb   to prepare an army for war, or to organize support for a cause

neutral

adjective   not taking part in nor supporting either side in a war

self-determination

noun   free choice over one's state without outside control

What happened to **isolationism**?

It ended. We're **mobilized** to fight for Britain and France.

 ## Other Useful Words

assume

verb   to guess that something is true

inform

verb   to tell someone facts or to share information

 ## Apply the Strategy

Look at a chapter in your textbook that your teacher identifies. Use familiar prefixes and suffixes to help you figure out the meaning of any new words you find.

Vocabulary: American History, SV 9781419035012

Name _____   Date _____

Finish the Sentence

Choose a word to finish each sentence. Write the correct word on the line.

1. Britain had many colonies, because the nation believed in _____.

isolationism   **immigration**   **imperialism**

2. The United States did not want to fight in World War I, because it believed in

_____.

isolationism   **immigration**   **imperialism**

3. Germany built a huge army because of _____.

isolationism   **militarism**   **reconstruction**

4. The Germans had strong feelings of _____ and believed their country

was the best.

militarism   **isolationism**   **nationalism**

5. Spain did not fight in World War I, because it was a _____ nation.

neutral   **frontier**   **armistice**

6. The United States _____ the army to send soldiers to Europe.

mobilized   **informed**   **imported**

7. The newspapers _____ readers that the war had ended.

informed   **assumed**   **converted**

8. Mom always cooked meatballs on special days, because she _____

it was my favorite food.

informed   **assumed**   **converted**

Name _____ Date _____

Word Challenge: True or False

Write **T** next to each sentence that is true. Write **F** next to each sentence that is false. Rewrite the false sentences. The first one has been done for you.

1. __F__ **Militarism** means an agreement to stop fighting.

   Militarism means to build an army.

2. _____ If a nation is **neutral**, it will fight in a war.

   _____

3. _____ **Imperialism** means building colonies and an empire.

   _____

4. _____ **Self-determination** means to organize soldiers for war.

   _____

Word Challenge: Which Word?

Think of a statement for each word below that gives a clue about its meaning. Write your statement next to the word. The first one has been done for you.

1. **inform** *"I share information."* _____

2. **isolationism** _____

3. **armistice** _____

4. **assume** _____

5. **mobilize** _____

Vocabulary: American History, SV 9781419035012

Name _____ Date _____

 Finish the Idea

Finish each idea to make a complete sentence. Write your answer on the line.

1. If you lived in a **neutral** nation, you might _____

_____

2. A nation would sign an **armistice** if _____

_____

3. I would **assume** you are happy if _____

_____

4. You would show feelings of **nationalism** if _____

_____

Word Study: The Suffix *-ize*

When you add *-ize* to an adjective such as *custom*, two things happen.
- The word becomes a verb: *customize*.
- The word now means to make something for one's own special taste.

custom (adj.) something made to personal order
customize (v.) to make something for one's own special taste

Add the suffix *-ize* to the words below. Write your own definition for each word. Use a dictionary to check your spelling and your definitions.

	+ *-ize*	Definition
1. mobile		
2. military		
3. neutral		
4. civil		
5. revolution		

Vocabulary: American History, SV 9781419035012

Name _____ Date _____

The Language of Testing

How would you answer a question like this on a test?

What was one **major cause** of World War I?

- Ⓐ imperialism
- Ⓑ slavery
- Ⓒ the search for gold
- Ⓓ emancipation

Tip

The word *cause* means the reason why something happened. The *major cause* is the most important reason why something happened.

Test Strategy: If a question asks for the major cause of something, restate the question using the phrase *most important reason for.* You can also add the phrase *is a major cause of* to each answer choice to test if it is right or wrong. For example, *imperialism* was a major cause of World War I.

1. How could you say the question above in a different way?

   _____

   _____

Try the strategy again by asking these questions in a different way. Also write what phrase you would use to test the answer choices.

2. Ana was an excellent student. What was the major cause for her success in school?

   - Ⓐ She wore nice clothes.
   - Ⓑ She had a cell phone.
   - Ⓒ She studied for every test.
   - Ⓓ She liked to sing.

   _____

   _____

   _____

   _____

3. Bob's new shoe store went out of business. What was the major cause of Bob's store closing?

   - Ⓐ Bob was very friendly.
   - Ⓑ The shoes cost too much money.
   - Ⓒ The shoes were beautiful.
   - Ⓓ The store had shoes and sneakers.

   _____

   _____

   _____

   _____

Lesson 12: World War I
Vocabulary: American History, SV 9781419035012

Name _____ Date _____

On Your Own

Answer the questions.

1. What are the benefits of an **armistice**? _____

   _____

2. How does **imperialism** change a country? _____

   _____

3. Why might a country have a policy of **isolationism**? _____

   _____

4. What are some features of **militarism**? _____

   _____

5. What might you **mobilize** your friends to do? _____

   _____

6. How do Americans show their **nationalism**? _____

   _____

7. What are some things you are **neutral** about? _____

   _____

8. Why might smaller countries want **self-determination**? _____

   _____

Write On!

You are a member of the Senate, and a debate is going on over whether or not the United States should adopt a policy of isolationism. On another sheet of paper, write a speech in which you state your views on isolationism. Be sure to give three or more examples or reasons to back up your opinion. Use four or more words from the lesson correctly in your speech.

nationalism	**militarism**	**imperialism**	**mobilize**	**neutral**
isolationism	**armistice**	**self-determination**	**inform**	**assume**

Name _____ Date _____

Lesson 12 Assessment

Read the sentences. Look for the best word to complete each sentence. Fill in the circle for the answer you choose. The first one has been done for you.

1. The people of Croatia declared their independence in 1991. This is an example of _____.
   - (A) nationalism
   - (B) imperialism
   - (C) self-determination
   - (D) isolationism

2. Japan withdrew from the League of Nations to build up its army. This is an example of _____.
   - (A) militarism
   - (B) imperialism
   - (C) isolationism
   - (D) armistice

3. Some people believe their country can do no wrong. This is an example of extreme _____.
   - (A) imperialism
   - (B) self-determination
   - (C) militarism
   - (D) nationalism

4. The treaty ending World War I is an example of _____.
   - (A) nationalism
   - (B) armistice
   - (C) isolationism
   - (D) militarism

5. Before the U.S. entered the war, Americans _____ supplies to send to Britain and France.
   - (A) assumed
   - (B) informed
   - (C) mobilized
   - (D) analyzed

6. Great Britain took over the country of South Africa. This is an example of _____.
   - (A) isolationism
   - (B) imperialism
   - (C) self-determination
   - (D) militarism

7. Switzerland is known as a _____ country because it has not taken sides during a war.
   - (A) neutral
   - (B) mobilized
   - (C) nativist
   - (D) progressive

8. Belinda _____ that John must have been sick since he was not in school today.
   - (A) informed
   - (B) assumed
   - (C) mobilized
   - (D) summarized

9. George Washington believed the U.S. should not become involved in the affairs of other countries. He believed in _____.
   - (A) self-determination
   - (B) militarism
   - (C) imperialism
   - (D) isolationism

10. The witness _____ the police detective of what she had seen at the crime scene.
    - (A) assumed
    - (B) mobilized
    - (C) informed
    - (D) portrayed

Lesson 12: World War I
Vocabulary: American History, SV 9781419035012

Between Two World Wars

Read the first passage below. Underline any examples or descriptions you find that might help you figure out the meaning of new words. Draw an arrow from the examples and descriptions to the word each describes. The first one has been done for you.

After World War I

After World War I, all the fighting nations signed a peace treaty. That treaty **specified**, or named, Germany as the nation that started the war. It also punished Germany for starting the war. Germany was forced to pay **reparations** <u>of billions of dollars to Britain and France.</u>

Many of the nations that fought wanted to prevent future wars. To do so, they followed a policy of **disarmament**. While the United States began making and owning fewer weapons, however, other countries like Germany began rebuilding their armies.

To many Americans, the 1920s were good years. Many people had more money and more time away from work. But some Americans were unhappy and left the United States. They settled in Europe and were called **expatriates**:

In 1919, the **Prohibition** Amendment was added to the Constitution. It said it was against the law to make or drink alcoholic beverages. It was impossible to carry out this law, however. In 1933, another amendment ended Prohibition forever.

Vocabulary Strategy

Look for definitions to help you understand the meanings of new words.

New American History Words

disarmament

noun when a nation makes and owns fewer weapons

expatriate

noun someone who has left his or her own country to live and work in another country

prohibition

noun the time during which something popular is made illegal, or the period in the United States when alcoholic beverages were illegal

reparation

noun money that a nation that has lost a war must pay the winning countries

...nd practice the strategy again. Underline the examples and
...aw an arrow from each to the word it describes.

... in America

...Americans
...Congress
...**otas**. The quotas
...ould come to
...ountries each year.
The quotas allowed fewer immigrants from
eastern and southern Europe.

In 1929, the Great **Depression** began.
The main events of the Great Depression
can be **sequenced** in the order that they
happened. First, the stock market crashed

and millions of people became poor. Second,
more and more people continued to lose
their jobs. Third, Franklin D. Roosevelt was
elected President. Fourth, the President
started new programs to end the Depression.

President Roosevelt started **relief**, or
help, programs for people who did not have
jobs. His programs gave jobs to millions of
people. The new programs made the United
States a **welfare** state. A welfare state
provides certain things to people when they
cannot find jobs.

✔ More New American History Words

depression

noun   a time when spending is low and many people do
not have jobs

quota

noun   a number that is a goal, like a limit on the number of
immigrants or how many items should be made or sold

relief

noun   help for serious problems

welfare

noun   happiness, health, and comfort, or money the
government gives people to help them survive

✔ Other Useful Words

sequence

noun   the order in which things should be

verb   to put things in order so that one thing comes
after another

specify

verb   to name something

💡 Apply the Strategy

Look at a chapter in
your textbook that your
teacher identifies. Use
examples, descriptions,
and pictures to help
you figure out the
meaning of any new
words you find.

Name _____ Date _____

Find the Word

Write a word from the box next to each clue. Then write the word made by the boxed letters to answer the question below.

| expatriates | welfare | depression | prohibition | quota |
| sequence | relief | disarmament | specify | reparations |

1. when people do not have jobs ___ ___ ___ ☐ ___ ___ ___ ___ ___

2. help for a serious problem ___ ☐ ___ ___ ___ ___

3. money paid by a country ___ ___ ☐ ___ ___ ___ ___ ___

4. to make fewer weapons ___ ___ ___ ☐ ___ ___ ___ ___

5. people who live and work in another

   country ___ ___ ___ ___ ☐ ___ ___ ___ ___

6. government money that helps people ___ ___ ___ ☐ ___ ___ ___

7. when something is illegal ___ ___ ___ ___ ☐ ___ ___ ___ ___

8. to name something ___ ___ ___ ☐ ___ ___

9. an amount that is a goal ___ ___ ☐ ___ ___

10. an order of events ___ ___ ___ ___ ☐ ___ ___ ___

What did Germany have to pay after World War I?

   It paid ___ ___ ___ ___ ___ ___ ___ ___ ___ ___ _S_ .

Lesson 13: Between Two World Wars
Vocabulary: American History, SV 9781419035012

Name _____ Date _____

Word Challenge: Word Association

Read the groups of words below. Write the word from the lesson that goes best with each group. The first one has been done for you.

1. __prohibition_____ not allowed, illegal, stop

2. _____ amount, limit, goal

3. _____ help, support, assistance

4. _____ place in order, set of events

5. _____ government money, help, well-being

Word Challenge: What's Your Reason?

Think of a reason for each statement and write it on the line. Write your reasons in complete sentences. The first one has been done for you.

1. It would have been hard to live during the Great **Depression**. __It was__ __hard because no one had any money to buy food._____

2. I would **specify** my favorite foods when visiting a friend for dinner. _____ _____

3. I would **sequence** the party pictures in the order that they were taken. _____

4. I feel **relief** at the end of the school year. _____ _____

Name _____ Date _____

Extend the Meaning

Write the letter of the word or phrase that best completes each sentence.

1. A country that wants **disarmament** would _____.
   a. build more weapons
   b build fewer weapons
   c. want a huge army

2. It is not possible to **sequence** _____.
   a. numbers
   b. dates
   c. pencils

3. During a **depression**, most people become _____.
   a. richer
   b. smarter
   c. poorer

4. An American **expatriate** might live in _____.
   a. New York
   b. California
   c. France

Word Study: The Suffix -ment

When the suffix -*ment* is added to a word like *settle,* two things happen.
- The suffix -*ment* changes a verb into a noun: *settlement.*
- The word now names the result or process of settling.

settle (v.) to set up a home somewhere
settlement (n.) a community built by people just moving into the area, or the process of moving into an area.

A. Add the suffix -*ment* to the words below. Write your own definition for each word. Use a dictionary to check your spelling and definitions.

	+ -*ment*	Definition
1. **achieve**		
2. **move**		
3. **ship**		
4. **develop**		

B. Complete each sentence with a word from the chart.

1. Roberto's excellent grades were an _____.

2. We could feel the _____ of the ship as we sailed.

Name _____ Date _____

The Language of Testing

How would you answer a question like this on a test?

The difficult times of the Great Depression
led to

    Ⓐ the beginning of World War I.

    Ⓑ too many people being out of work.

    Ⓒ new libraries being built.

    Ⓓ Americans moving to China.

Tip

The phrase *led to* tells you that you need to find a result of the event in the question.

Test Strategy: Always read the whole question and all the answers first. Then if the question has the phrase *led to*, reword the question to ask for a result of the event in the question.

1. How could you say the question above in a different way?

_____

_____

Try the strategy again by asking these questions in a different way.

2. Paul's job in a summer camp led to

    Ⓐ an interest in becoming a teacher.

    Ⓑ a dislike for horses.

    Ⓒ being afraid of dogs.

    Ⓓ learning to cook.

3. Germany's defeat in World War I led to

    Ⓐ fifty years of peace.

    Ⓑ more trips to Germany.

    Ⓒ Germany paying reparations.

    Ⓓ the building of new museums.

Lesson 13: Between Two World Wars
Vocabulary: American History, SV 9781419035012

On Your Own

Answer the questions.

1. What can cause a **depression**? _____
   _____

2. What happens during a **disarmament**? _____
   _____

3. Why might someone become an **expatriate**? _____
   _____

4. What are some **prohibitions** you follow at school? _____
   _____

5. How can you make sure you reach your **quota** of sleep each night? _____
   _____

6. What organizations provide **relief** to people who have suffered? _____
   _____

7. What might a group receive **reparations** for? _____
   _____

8. How does **welfare** help people? _____
   _____

Write On!

You are one of Franklin D. Roosevelt's advisors during his first term as president. On another sheet of paper, write a memo in which you recommend three or more things that he should do to aid the American people during the Great Depression. Be sure to include why you are recommending each action. Use four or more words from the lesson correctly in your memo.

reparation	**disarmament**	**expatriate**	**prohibition**	**quota**
depression	**sequence**	**welfare**	**specify**	**relief**

Name _____ Date _____

Lesson 13 Assessment

Read the sentences. Look for the best word to complete each sentence. Fill in the circle for the answer you choose. The first one has been done for you.

1. The Declaration of Independence _____ that all people are created equal.
   - Ⓐ assumes
   - Ⓑ specifies
   - Ⓒ sequences
   - Ⓓ speculates

2. Many well-known writers became _____ by moving from the United States to Paris in the 1920s.
   - Ⓐ reparations
   - Ⓑ prohibitions
   - Ⓒ quotas
   - Ⓓ expatriates

3. The Comprehensive Nuclear Test Ban Treaty is an example of a policy of _____.
   - Ⓐ disarmament
   - Ⓑ response
   - Ⓒ reparation
   - Ⓓ welfare

4. In 1987, the stock market crashed like it did in 1929. However, this time there was not a severe _____.
   - Ⓐ prohibition
   - Ⓑ relief
   - Ⓒ depression
   - Ⓓ reparation

5. Social Security is an example of a government _____ program.
   - Ⓐ reparation
   - Ⓑ disarmament
   - Ⓒ welfare
   - Ⓓ quota

6. The _____ of events that led up to the Great Depression ended with the stock market crash of 1929.
   - Ⓐ sequence
   - Ⓑ quota
   - Ⓒ welfare
   - Ⓓ relief

7. Sometimes a country that has lost a war does not have to make _____.
   - Ⓐ quotas
   - Ⓑ reparations
   - Ⓒ welfare
   - Ⓓ relief

8. In 1924, a government act set an immigration _____ of 165,000 new people into the United States.
   - Ⓐ expatriate
   - Ⓑ reparation
   - Ⓒ disarmament
   - Ⓓ quota

9. After the devastating tsunami on December 26, 2004, the United States sent millions of dollars in _____ to the countries affected.
   - Ⓐ relief
   - Ⓑ quotas
   - Ⓒ reparations
   - Ⓓ expatriates

10. Many gangsters made money during _____ by selling illegal beverages.
    - Ⓐ reparation
    - Ⓑ disarmament
    - Ⓒ the Depression
    - Ⓓ Prohibition

World War II

Read the passage below. Think about the meanings of the new words printed in **bold**. Circle any familiar root words inside the new words that might help you figure out what these words mean. The first one has been done for you.

World War II Begins

A **survey** of the 1930s and 1940s tells us that these were difficult years in Europe. Italy and Germany had governments that were based on ideas of **fascism**. Under fascism, powerful leaders had strong armies and full control of the government.

The governments of Italy, Germany, the Soviet Union, and Japan were also based on the ideas of **totalitarianism**. These governments had total control over the lives of every person. People who spoke out against the government were killed.

Adolf Hitler became the fascist leader of Germany. In 1936, he began taking control of different countries in Europe. At first, Britain and France followed a policy of **appeasement**, or giving in, to Hitler. World War II began in 1939 when Hitler's army attacked Poland. Britain and France fought against Hitler as Poland's **allies**, or friends. However, Hitler quickly won control of Poland.

There was a quick increase, or **escalation**, in fighting. Hitler won control of many other countries, including France.

Vocabulary Strategy

Use words you know to help unlock unfamiliar words in the family. For example, *total* can help you unlock the meaning of *totalitarianism*.

Adolf Hitler

Harmon Foundation Collection, National Archives

New American History Words

ally

noun a person or country that agrees to support another

appeasement

noun the act of giving in to a person or country to have peace

escalation

noun a sudden and large increase

fascism

noun a government that controls the lives of people, targets certain groups, and builds a large army

totalitarianism

noun a form of government, such as fascism, that has total control over the lives of people

Name _____ Date _____

Now read the passage below and practice the vocabulary strategy again. Circle familiar root words that are found in larger, unfamiliar words.

Winning World War II

On December 7, 1941, Japan bombed American ships at Pearl Harbor in Hawaii and killed more than 2,000 Americans. After that, the United States went to war against Japan, Germany, and Italy. In 1942, all Japanese Americans on the West Coast were ordered to move to **internment** camps. These camps were heavily guarded.

The United States and its allies defeated Germany, Italy, and Japan in 1945. The world soon learned about the **Holocaust**, or the organized killing of six million Jews in Europe. As Hitler captured different countries, Jews and other people were sent to death camps. Hitler carefully planned this **genocide** against the Jews.

At the end of World War II, American soldiers started the **liberation** of the camps. However, it was too late to save the millions who had already been killed.

More New American History Words

genocide

noun   the killing of an entire race or group

Holocaust

noun   the murder of six million Jews by Hitler during World War II

noun   total or near total destruction of life

internment

noun   the act of forcing people to stay in one place, such as a prison or a guarded space

liberation

noun   the act of freeing people

Apply the Strategy

Look at a chapter in your textbook that your teacher identifies. Use familiar root words to help you figure out the meaning of any new words you find.

Other Useful Words

highlight

verb   to show that something is important

noun   an important time during an event

survey

noun   the information that is gathered about a topic

verb   to collect information about a topic

Vocabulary: American History, SV 9781419035012

Name _____   Date _____

Finish the Sentence

Use a word from the box to finish each sentence. Write the correct word on the line.

survey	genocide	appeasement	escalation	fascism

1. The form of government in which a leader uses the army to control the country is

   _____.

2. A _____ was made before the election to find out how people planned

   to vote.

3. More and more soldiers died because of the _____ in fighting.

4. Tommy's mother let him eat too many cookies because she hoped _____

   would stop him from fighting with his brother.

5. Hitler committed _____ against many groups, including the Jews.

Holocaust	Totalitarianism	liberated	internment	highlight

6. Jenna uses a yellow marker to _____ important ideas as she reads.

7. Japanese Americans were forced into _____ camps during World War II.

8. The killing of six million Jews during World War II was the _____.

9. _____ means a government has total control over the lives of people.

10. The death camps were _____ at the end of the war.

Vocabulary: American History, SV 9781419035012

Name _____ Date _____

Word Challenge: What's Your Answer?

Read each question and write an answer on the line. Answer questions in complete sentences. The first one has been done for you.

1. Why would you not want to live under **fascism**? _I would not like to live_ _under fascism because I like having freedom._

2. What would you **highlight** in your history book? _____

_____

3. What could you learn if you took a **survey** in your school? _____

_____

4. Why is **genocide** very wrong? _____

_____

Word Challenge: True or False

Write **T** next to each sentence that is true. Write **F** next to each sentence that is false. Rewrite the false sentences. The first one has been done for you.

1. __F__ **Holocaust** is the name of a fascist leader.

   The Holocaust was the murder of six million Jews during WW II.

2. _____ Under **totalitarianism**, a government has total control over people's lives.

   _____

3. _____ **Liberation** means that people must stay in prison.

   _____

4. _____ **Escalation** means there would be less fighting during a war.

   _____

Vocabulary: American History, SV 9781419035012

Name _____ Date _____

Synonyms and Antonyms

Look at each group of words. Circle two words in each group that are synonyms or two words in each group that are antonyms. Then write whether the circled words are synonyms or antonyms on the line below each group.

1. liberation   suffrage

    neutral   freedom

    _____

2. escalation   lowering

    compromise   slavery

    _____

3. survey   region

    study   duties

    _____

4. highlight   canal

    charter   emphasize

    _____

Word Study: Compound Words

A compound word is a word that is made when two words are joined together. The new word often has a completely new meaning from the words it contains.

birth + place = birthplace
fire + works = fireworks

A. Complete the chart.

	Compound Word	Definition
1. high + light		
2. sky + scraper		
3. home + land		

B. Complete each sentence with a compound word from the chart.

1. Alexandra's _____ is in Mexico, and she has always lived there.

2. The tall _____ had more than 100 floors.

     Lesson 14: World War II
Vocabulary: American History, SV 9781419035012

The Language of Testing

How would you answer a question like this on a test?

What would be the best title for a newspaper story about the internment of Japanese Americans during World War II?

- (A) Japanese Americans Live in California
- (B) Japanese Americans Are Unfairly Sent to Internment Camps
- (C) Japanese Americans Shop for Food
- (D) Japanese Americans Move to China

Tip

The phrase *what would be the best title* means you must think of the most important idea about the topic.

Test Strategy: If the question asks *what would be the best title*, ask yourself which of the four choices shows the most important idea about the topic. That will be the correct answer for the question.

Try the strategy again with these questions. Circle the best answer and write a sentence to explain your choice.

1. What would be the best title for an article about the celebration of Thanksgiving?

- (A) Too Many Fish
- (B) Too Far to Drive
- (C) A Holiday for All Americans
- (D) No School on Thursday

_____

_____

_____

_____

_____

2. What would be the best title for an article about U.S. entry into World War II?

- (A) The United States Enters the War After Pearl Harbor
- (B) Hitler Speaks to Germany
- (C) Fascism in Italy
- (D) Not Enough Food

_____

_____

_____

_____

_____

115
Lesson 14: World War II
Vocabulary: American History, SV 9781419035012

Name _____ Date _____

 On Your Own

Answer the questions.

1. Who is your greatest **ally**? _____

_____

2. Describe an act of **appeasement** you have seen or performed. _____

_____

3. How can you stop the **escalation** of an argument? _____

_____

4. What are some features of **fascism**? _____

_____

5. What makes people commit **genocide**? _____

_____

6. What was the **Holocaust**? _____

_____

7. What happens to people during **internment**? _____

_____

8. What power does a common citizen have under **totalitarianism**? Why? _____

_____

Write On!

You are a member of the U.S. forces taking part in the liberation of concentration camps. On another sheet of paper, write a letter to your family back home in which you describe three or more things that you see and how they make you feel. Use four or more words from the lesson correctly in your letter.

internment	**highlight**	**appeasement**	**escalation**	**fascism**	**ally**
Holocaust	**liberation**	**totalitarianism**	**genocide**	**survey**	

Vocabulary: American History, SV 9781419035012

Name _____   Date _____

Lesson 14 Assessment

Read the sentences. Look for the best word to complete each sentence. Fill in the circle for the answer you choose. The first one has been done for you.

1. The students hoped to _____ the school bully so he wouldn't pick on them anymore.
   - (A) liberate
   - (B) highlight
   - (C) survey
   - (D) appease

2. The United States and England are now _____ that help each other out in times of need.
   - (A) highlights
   - (B) allies
   - (C) republics
   - (D) expatriates

3. Other people, such as Roma and Communists, were also killed during the _____.
   - (A) liberation
   - (B) appeasement
   - (C) Holocaust
   - (D) expatriates

4. A government that has total control over its citizens is an example of _____.
   - (A) totalitarianism
   - (B) genocide
   - (C) militarism
   - (D) imperialism

5. _____ has killed nearly 800,000 Tutsi people in Rwanda.
   - (A) Internment
   - (B) Genocide
   - (C) Liberation
   - (D) Escalation

6. The _____ of the concentration camps brought freedom to the prisoners.
   - (A) genocide
   - (B) internment
   - (C) appeasement
   - (D) liberation

7. The group had an unofficial _____ to see how voters felt about the candidate.
   - (A) highlight
   - (B) Holocaust
   - (C) genocide
   - (D) survey

8. The _____ of crime in the city caused the mayor to hire more police officers.
   - (A) escalation
   - (B) internment
   - (C) genocide
   - (D) liberation

9. After the bombing of Pearl Harbor, Japanese Americans were moved to _____ camps.
   - (A) liberation
   - (B) genocide
   - (C) internment
   - (D) totalitarianism

10. The _____ government of Italy during World War II allowed the Italian people no freedom.
    - (A) appeasement
    - (B) fascist
    - (C) escalation
    - (D) internment

Vocabulary: American History, SV 9781419035012

Name _____ Date _____

The Cold War to the Present

Read the passage below. Think about the meanings of the words printed in **bold**. Underline any definitions that might help you figure out what these words mean. The first one has been done for you.

The Cold War Years

The Cold War began in 1945. It was a struggle between the United States and the Soviet Union.

The Soviet Union had a totalitarian government that followed the ideas of **communism**. Under communism, the government owns all land and businesses. The Soviet Union wanted to spread communism to other countries. The United States responded with a policy of **containment**. This policy means working to stop the spread of communism.

Today, when people **review**, or study, the Cold War years, they learn that Americans worried about the spread of communism. They also worried that the Soviet Union would attack America with **nuclear** weapons. Both nations had nuclear weapons, however, and they agreed to not use them.

During the 1950s, African Americans worked to end **discrimination**, or unfair treatment because of race. Through many protests and battles, African Americans slowly won equal rights.

 New American History Words

communism

noun a system of government in which the government controls all businesses, or an economy in which there is no government and the people share the wealth

containment

noun the policy of working to stop the spread of something

discrimination

noun the unfair treatment of people because of their race, age, religion, or other factors

nuclear

adjective powered by the energy that is given off by splitting atoms

www.harcourtschoolsupply.com
118
Lesson 15: The Cold War to the Present
Vocabulary: American History, SV 9781419035012

Name _____ Date _____

Now read this passage and practice the vocabulary strategy again. Underline any definitions in the passage that help you figure out what the new words in **bold** mean.

Some Problems in Today's World

The United States has a huge **deficit**. A deficit means the government spends more money than it takes in.

The United States has fought two wars against the Middle East country of Iraq. During the 1990s, American leaders believed Iraq was building very dangerous weapons. **Sanctions** were placed against Iraq. This means nations could not trade with Iraq. In 2003, the United States and Great Britain went to war against Iraq. Iraq's leader, Saddam Hussein, was removed from power. The sanctions were lifted. Iraq could trade with other nations again. But problems in Iraq still continue.

Terrorism is a world problem. The worst act of terrorism in the United States happened on September 11, 2001. Terrorists attacked the World Trade Center in New York City and the Pentagon building in Washington, D.C. More than 3,000 people were killed. People everywhere **related** to the pain felt by the victims and their families. President George W. Bush promised there would be **retaliation**, or fighting back.

More New American History Words

deficit

noun the government's spending of more money than it takes in

retaliation

noun the act of taking action against a person or country that has hurt you

sanctions

noun a decision to stop trade with a nation that has caused problems

terrorism

noun unpredictable acts of violence against innocent people to make a statement

Of course there's a **deficit**. You're spending more than you make.

Other Useful Words

relate

verb to feel connected to or to respond to something

review

verb to study or examine something

noun the act of studying or analyzing something

Apply the Strategy

Look at a chapter in your textbook that your teacher identifies. Use definitions in the text to help you figure out the meaning of any new words you find.

Name _____ Date _____

 Finish the Sentence

Choose a word to finish each sentence. Write the correct word on the line.

1. The _____ weapons are very, very dangerous.

   survey   **nuclear**   **review**

2. People who live under _____ are not allowed to have their own businesses.

   republic   **communism**   **mercantilism**

3. A good student always _____ before a test.

   reviews   **expands**   **sequences**

4. If you spend more money than you earn, you will have a _____.

   sanction   **review**   **deficit**

5. Dan did not do well in sports, so he could _____ to other people who were also not good athletes.

   review   **relate**   **retaliate**

6. The United States had a policy of _____ against communism.

   containment   **quota**   **terrorism**

7. The attacks on the World Trade Center and the Pentagon on September 11, 2001, were an example of _____.

   deficit   **terrorism**   **communism**

8. African Americans faced _____ when they were not allowed to buy houses in white neighborhoods.

   liberation   **discrimination**   **depression**

9. Many nations did not trade with Iraq because of _____ against that country.

   surveys   **reviews**   **sanctions**

10. The United States attacked terrorist bases in _____ for the World Trade Center attacks.

   retaliation   **liberation**   **escalation**

Name _____ Date _____

World Challenge: Which Word?

Think of a statement for each word below that gives a clue about its meaning. Write your statement next to the word. The first one has been done for you.

1. **deficit** _"I am a problem with money."_

2. **communism** _____

3. **discrimination** _____

4. **retaliation** _____

Word Challenge: Think About It

Write a sentence to answer each question. The first one has been done for you.

1. African Americans faced **discrimination** when they applied for jobs. Do you think they were treated fairly? _No. Everyone should have the same chances to get a job._

2. Sam did not **review** for his test. How do you think Sam did on the test?
   _____
   _____

3. The U.S. government has **sanctions** against a certain country. How do you think the U.S. government feels about that country? _____
   _____

4. Meena **relates** to Sung because he hates big parties. Do you think Meena would rather go to a large party or a small one? _____
   _____

Name _____ Date _____

Finish the Idea

Finish each idea to make a complete sentence. Write your answers on the line.

1. I would work to end **discrimination** because _____

_____

2. **Communism** is different from capitalism because _____

_____

3. A **deficit** can be a problem because _____

_____

4. **Nuclear** weapons are dangerous because _____

_____

Word Study: The Suffix -ed

The suffix -ed changes a verb to the past tense.
- Present tense: Peter *reviews* the lesson.
- Past tense: Martha *reviewed* the lesson.

The suffix -ed is added only to verbs.
When -ed is added to a verb that ends in y, change the y to i and then add -ed.
  inform = informed
  specify = specified

A. Complete the chart.

Present Tense	+ -ed	Definition
1. review		
2. contain		
3. discriminate		
4. specify		

B. Use a past tense word from the chart to finish each sentence.

1. When I ordered the sandwich, I _____ that I wanted whole wheat bread.

2. The small box _____ a beautiful watch.

Name _____   Date _____

How would you answer a question like this on a test?

Which point of view did the U.S. government have about communism during the Cold War?

Ⓐ Communism is good for poor people.
Ⓑ All people in Europe should follow communism.
Ⓒ We should contain communism.
Ⓓ Communism will soon end.

Tip
The phrase *which point of view* means you must decide on the point of view of one person or group. Different people or groups will often have different points of view about the same event.

Test Strategy: Always begin by reading the full question and all of the possible answers. Then think of at least two different points of view for the same event. Decide on the one point of view from the answer group that is probably held by the person or group named in the question.

Try the strategy again with these questions. Circle the answer you think is correct. Write a sentence to explain why you chose your answer.

1. The school principal said students will fail if they miss more than ten days of school. The principal's point of view is that

Ⓐ students can learn well at home.
Ⓑ too many students are promoted.
Ⓒ school attendance is important.
Ⓓ students should ride bikes.

2. What was President George W. Bush's point of view about the terrorist attacks on September 11, 2001?

Ⓐ We should forget about the attacks.
Ⓑ We should retaliate.
Ⓒ We cannot prevent terrorism.
Ⓓ The attacks were an accident.

_____
_____
_____
_____
_____
_____

_____
_____
_____
_____
_____
_____

www.harcourtschoolsupply.com
123
Lesson 15: The Cold War to the Present
Vocabulary: American History, SV 9781419035012

Name _____ Date _____

On Your Own

Answer the questions.

1. How is **communism** different from capitalism? _____

   _____

2. What is the purpose of **containment**? _____

   _____

3. How does a **deficit** happen? _____

   _____

4. What kinds of **discrimination** are there? _____

   _____

5. What are some things that can be described as **nuclear**? _____

   _____

6. What are some kinds of **retaliation**? _____

   _____

7. How might **sanctions** harm a country? _____

   _____

8. What are some of the effects of **terrorism**? _____

   _____

Write On!

What do you see as the greatest problem facing the United States today? Pick an issue such as terrorism, health care, energy, environmental issues, or the budget deficit. On another sheet of paper, write a short essay explaining why you think it is such a big problem. Be sure to give plenty of examples to support your opinion, and use four or more words from the lesson correctly in your essay.

communism	containment	nuclear	discrimination	deficit
sanctions	terrorism	retaliation	review	relate

www.harcourtschoolsupply.com
124
Lesson 15: The Cold War to the Present
Vocabulary: American History, SV 9781419035012

Lesson 15 Assessment

Read the sentences. Look for the best word to complete each sentence.
Fill in the circle for the answer you choose. The first one has been done for you.

1. In 1963, the U.S. placed _____ on Cuba in response to hostile actions by the Cuban government. They still exist today.
   - Ⓐ containment
   - Ⓑ retaliation
   - Ⓒ sanctions
   - Ⓓ discrimination

2. The United States often runs a budget _____ of billions of dollars.
   - Ⓐ deficit
   - Ⓑ containment
   - Ⓒ retaliation
   - Ⓓ sanctions

3. Tearing down the Berlin Wall symbolized the end of _____ in Eastern Europe.
   - Ⓐ sanctions
   - Ⓑ communism
   - Ⓒ discrimination
   - Ⓓ containment

4. Each year, the U.S. government _____ its budget to see if it can cut expenses.
   - Ⓐ relates
   - Ⓑ specifies
   - Ⓒ reviews
   - Ⓓ abbreviates

5. In 1986, the United States bombed several locations in Libya in _____ for its support of terrorist organizations.
   - Ⓐ containment
   - Ⓑ sanctions
   - Ⓒ discrimination
   - Ⓓ retaliation

6. The electricity that keeps the lights on in many homes comes from _____ energy.
   - Ⓐ terrorism
   - Ⓑ nuclear
   - Ⓒ retaliation
   - Ⓓ containment

7. Many New Yorkers who witnessed the terrorist attacks in 2001 could _____ to Londoners after the subway bombings in 2005.
   - Ⓐ relate
   - Ⓑ review
   - Ⓒ analyze
   - Ⓓ emphasize

8. African Americans fought hard against _____ and for equal rights.
   - Ⓐ sanctions
   - Ⓑ discrimination
   - Ⓒ containment
   - Ⓓ retaliation

9. The Truman Doctrine specified that the U.S. would support countries that were fighting communism. This is one example of how the U.S. exercised its policy of _____.
   - Ⓐ retaliation
   - Ⓑ sanctions
   - Ⓒ containment
   - Ⓓ discrimination

10. An airplane was blown up by explosives that were snuck on board. This disaster was an act of _____.
    - Ⓐ communism
    - Ⓑ terrorism
    - Ⓒ sanctions
    - Ⓓ containment

Answer Key

page 8
1. D   4. A   7. J   10. I
2. E   5. B   8. F
3. C   6. H   9. G

page 9
Word Challenge:
What's Your Reason?
Answers will vary.
Word Challenge:
What's Your Answer?
Answers will vary.

page 10
Finish the Sentence
1. domesticated
2. speculated
3. artifact
4. region
5. migration
Word Study
1. societal; adjective, relating to a society
2. environmental; adjective, relating to the environment
3. cultural; adjective, relating to a culture
4. regional; adjective, relating to a certain region

page 11
Answers to restated questions will vary.
Check students' responses.
1. B   2. C   3. C

page 12
Answers will vary.

page 13
1. C   4. B   7. D   10. B
2. B   5. D   8. C
3. A   6. B   9. A

page 16
1. border
2. convert
3. objectives
4. missionaries
5. empire
6. settlement
7. charter
8. confirmed
9. exchanged
10. plantations

page 17
Word Challenge:
Would You Rather . . .
Answers will vary.
Word Challenge:
Quick Pick
1. A river, because it can

separate two states or countries.
2. A charter would give you permission to build a town.
3. A missionary would teach religion.
4. People would build houses when they start a settlement.

page 18
The Right Word
1. plantation   4. confirm
2. objective   5. convert
3. border
Word Study
1. unconverted
2. adjective, not proven true
3. unsettled, not settled or stable

page 19
Answers to restated questions will vary.
Check students' responses.
1. C   2. B   3. A

page 20
Answers will vary.

page 21
1. B   4. C   7. C   10. C
2. D   5. A   8. A
3. B   6. D   9. D

page 24
1. pilgrim
2. dissenter
3. covenant
4. predict
5. proprietor
6. rebellion
7. sect
8. indicate
9. colony
10. indentured
Puzzle answer: proprietor

page 25
Word Challenge:
Correct or Incorrect?
1. C
2. I; An indentured worker is not paid for his or her work.
3. I; Life was full of fighting during the rebellion.
4. C
Word Challenge:
Finish the Idea
Answers will vary.

page 26
Extend the Meaning
1. a   2. c   3. a   4. a
Word Study
1. dissenter, noun, a person who disagrees
2. indicator, noun, a tool that shows some kind of fact
3. settler, noun, a person who moves into an area and begins a community
4. planter, noun, a person or tool that plants things

page 27
Answers to restated questions will vary.
Check students' responses.
Ex. C
1. A   2. C

page 28
Answers will vary.

page 29
1. B   4. C   7. A   10. B
2. D   5. B   8. C
3. A   6. D   9. D

page 32
1. agriculture
2. staple
3. apprentice
4. duties
5. mercantilism
6. emphasized
7. import
8. export

page 33
Word Challenge:
Word Association
1. agriculture
2. expand
3. duties
4. emphasize
5. enterprise
Word Challenge:
Example/Not an Example
Answers will vary.

page 34
Analogies
1. apprentice
2. expand
3. agriculture
4. export
Word Study
A. 1. port; to move from one place to another
2. port; movable
3. port; someone who moves something

B. 1. porter
2. transportation
3. portable

page 35
Ex. B
Students should cross out *illustrate* and write *mean*.
1. Students should cross out B, C, and D.
2. Students should cross out A, C, and D.

page 36
Answers will vary.

page 37
1. D   4. B   7. D   10. A
2. B   5. A   8. D
3. C   6. C   9. B

page 40
1. assembly
2. tariff
3. boycotted
4. debate
5. organize
6. intolerance
7. repeal
8. militia

page 41
Word Challenge:
Finish the Idea
Answers will vary.
Word Challenge:
What's Your Answer?
Answers will vary.

page 42
Synonyms or Antonyms
1. boycott, buy; antonyms
2. intolerance, disapproval; synonyms
3. tariff, tax; synonyms
4. assembly, lawmakers; synonyms
Word Study
A. 1. impossible; not capable of being done or happening
2. inexperienced; not having experience, knowledge, or skill
3. inconvenient; not easy to do, use, or get to
4. indirect; not straightforward
B. 1. impossible
2. inconvenient

page 43
Answers to restated questions will vary.
Check students' responses.
1. D   2. C   3. B

Vocabulary: American History, SV 9781419035012

page 44
Answers will vary.

page 45
1. D   4. A   7. D   10. D
2. B   5. C   8. A
3. C   6. B   9. B

page 48
1. B   3. A   5. G   7. H
2. D   4. C   6. E   8. F

page 49
Word Challenge:
Would You Rather . . .
Answers will vary.
Word Challenge:
Quick Pick
Answers will vary.

page 50
Finish the Idea
Answers will vary.
Word Study
A. 1. location; a place
   2. proposition; a plan or suggestion
   3. revolution; the overthrow of a government
B. 1. location
   2. proposition

page 51
Answers to restated questions will vary.
Check students' responses.
1. D   2. D   3. C

page 52
Answers will vary.

page 53
1. C   4. A   7. C   10. B
2. C   5. B   8. B
3. D   6. D   9. D

page 56
1. executive
2. legislate
3. judicial
4. republic
5. amendment
6. federalism
7. representatives
8. sovereignty
9. define
10. omit

page 57
Word Challenge:
Definitions
1. Yes. A republic is a nation that has a prime minister or president as its leader.
2. Yes. Sentences will vary.
3. Yes. Sentences will vary.
4. No. Sovereignty means that a nation can control its own government.
Word Challenge:
What's Your Answer?
Answers will vary.

page 58
Analogies
1. legislate   3. define
2. omit   4. judicial
Word Study
A. 1. federalism; a federal system of government
   2. colonialism; control by one power over another area or people
   3. agriculturalism; a way of life depending on farming and crops
   4. loyalism; being loyal to a certain government
B. 1. loyalism
   2. colonialism

page 59
Answers to restated questions will vary.
Check students' responses.
1. C   2. C   3. C

page 60
Answers will vary.

page 61
1. D   4. B   7. A   10. B
2. B   5. C   8. C
3. A   6. B   9. D

page 64
1. illustrate
2. expedition
3. expansion
4. removal
5. describe
6. illustrate
7. territory
8. pioneer
9. frontier
10. canal
Puzzle answer: expedition

page 65
Word Challenge:
Word Association
1. pioneers
2. expedition
3. territory
4. expansion
5. illustrate
Word Challenge:
Would You Rather . . .
Answers will vary.

page 66
Extend the Meaning
1. c   2. b   3. b   4. c

Word Study
1. remove; to take off or do away with
2. removable; able to be taken off or done away with
3. movement; a motion or action of a person or group
4. immovable; not able to be moved or changed

page 67
Answers to restated questions will vary.
Check students' responses.
1. C   2. B   3. A

page 68
Answers will vary.

page 69
1. D   4. C   7. C   10. B
2. C   5. B   8. A
3. A   6. D   9. C

page 72
1. slavery
2. abolition
3. seceded
4. Confederacy
5. Reconstruction
6. emancipation
7. amnesty
8. compromised

page 73
Word Challenge:
Think About It
Answers will vary.
Word Challenge:
What's Your Answer?
Answers will vary.

page 74
Synonyms or Antonyms
1. emancipation, freedom; synonyms
2. summarize, lengthen; antonyms
3. compromise, agreement; synonyms
4. reconstruction, rebuild; synonyms
Word Study
A. 1. verb; organize something again
   2. both; order something again, something that has been ordered again
   3. verb; construct something again
B. 1. reorder
   2. reorganize

page 75
Answers to restated questions will vary.
Check students' responses.
1. C   2. B   3. B

page 76
Answers will vary.

page 77
1. A   4. C   7. A   10. D
2. D   5. B   8. C
3. B   6. D   9. B

page 80
1. C   4. E   7. G   10. H
2. A   5. D   8. J
3. B   6. I   9. F

page 81
Word Challenge:
Would You Rather . . .
Answers will vary.
Word Challenge:
Finish the Idea
Answers will vary.

page 82
Extend the Meaning
1. b   2. b   3. a   4. c
Word Study
A. 1. predictable; can be predicted
   2. describable; can be described
   3. expandable; can be expanded
   4. confirmable; can be confirmed
B. Answers will vary.

page 83
Answers to restated questions will vary.
Check students' responses.
1. B   2. B   3. A

page 84
Answers will vary.

page 85
1. C   4. B   7. B   10. C
2. B   5. A   8. A
3. A   6. D   9. D

page 88
1. immigration
2. nativists
3. socialism
4. progressives
5. analyzed
6. responded
7. conservation
8. suffrage
9. segregation
10. integration

Vocabulary: American History, SV 9781419035012

page 89
Word Challenge:
What's Your Answer?
Answers will vary.
Word Challenge:
Word Associations
1. progressive
2. socialism
3. segregation
4. conservation
5. nativist

page 90
Finish the Idea
Answers will vary.
Word Study
A. 1. expensive; high-priced
   2. repulsive; causing strong dislike
   3. attractive; having the power to attract; pretty
B. 1. attractive
   2. repulsive
   3. expensive

page 91
Answers to restated questions will vary.
Check students' responses.
1. A   2. C   3. B

page 92
Answers will vary.

page 93
1. A   4. C   7. C   10. B
2. C   5. D   8. D
3. A   6. B   9. C

page 96
1. imperialism
2. isolationism
3. militarism
4. nationalism
5. neutral
6. mobilized
7. informed
8. assumed

page 97
Word Challenge:
True or False
1. F; Militarism means to build an army.
2. F; If a nation is neutral, it will not fight in a war.
3. T
4. F; Self-determination means to have free choice over one's state without outside control.
Word Challenge:
Which Word?
Answers will vary.

page 98
Finish the Idea
Answers will vary.
Word Study
1. mobilize; to put into motion
2. militarize; to prepare for war
3. neutralize; to make neutral
4. civilize; to improve in habits or manners
5. revolutionize; to make a complete change

page 99
Answers to restated questions will vary.
Check students' responses.
1. A   2. C   3. B

page 100
Answers will vary.

page 101
1. C   4. B   7. A   10. C
2. A   5. C   8. B
3. D   6. B   9. D

page 104
1. depression
2. relief
3. reparations
4. disarmament
5. expatriates
6. welfare
7. prohibition
8. specify
9. quota
10. sequence
Puzzle answer: reparations

page 105
Word Challenge:
Word Association
1. prohibition
2. quota
3. relief
4. sequence
5. welfare
Word Challenge:
What's Your Reason?
Answers will vary.

page 106
Extend the Meaning
1. b   2. c   3. c   4. c
Word Study
A. 1. achievement; the act of being successful at something
   2. movement; a motion or action of a person or group
   3. shipment; the shipping or transporting of goods
   4. development; a step or stage in growth; advancement
B. 1. achievement
   2. movement

page 107
Answers to restated questions will vary.
Check students' responses.
1. B   2. A   3. C

page 108
Answers will vary.

page 109
1. B   4. C   7. B   10. D
2. D   5. C   8. D
3. A   6. A   9. A

page 112
1. fascism
2. survey
3. escalation
4. appeasement
5. genocide
6. highlight
7. internment
8. Holocaust
9. Totalitarianism
10. liberated

page 113
Word Challenge:
What's Your Answer?
Answers will vary.
Word Challenge:
True or False
1. F; The Holocaust was the murder of six million Jews during WWII.
2. T
3. F; Liberation means that people are free.
4. F; Escalation means there would be more fighting during a war.

page 114
Synonyms and Antonyms
1. liberation, freedom; synonyms
2. escalation, lowering; antonyms
3. survey, study; synonyms
4. highlight, emphasize; synonyms
Word Study
A. 1. highlight; to give importance to
   2. skyscraper; a very tall building
   3. homeland; the country where someone was born or the country someone lives in
B. 1. homeland
   2. skyscraper

page 115
Answers to restated questions will vary.
Check students' responses.
1. B   2. C   3. A

page 116
Answers will vary.

page 117
1. D   4. A   7. D   10. B
2. B   5. B   8. A
3. C   6. D   9. C

page 120
1. nuclear
2. communism
3. reviews
4. deficit
5. relate
6. containment
7. terrorism
8. discrimination
9. sanctions
10. retaliation

page 121
Word Challenge:
Which Word?
Answers will vary.
Word Challenge:
Think About It
Answers will vary.

page 122
Finish the Idea
Answers will vary.
Word Study
A. 1. reviewed; looked over or read again
   2. contained; held in
   3. discriminated; showed prejudice against or preference for something or someone
   4. specified; described in detail, made clear
B. 1. specified
   2. contained

page 123
Answers to restated questions will vary.
Check students' responses.
Ex. C
1. C   2. B

page 124
Answers will vary.

page 125
1. C   4. C   7. A   10. B
2. A   5. D   8. B
3. B   6. B   9. C

Vocabulary: American History, SV 9781419035012